Final Countdown:

I invented a source of energy that can be placed in the basement of every home or apartment complex or business address. This is how it works. You take a three foot wide and six foot long and 6 inch deep inset case of lead and on either side of the inner case you place a uranium isotope battery with a tiny amount of rads in the each six foot scale AA batteries of lead gilding. One battery to the left side of the inset case and one on the right side of the case, with both batteries at top as positive poles. The charge flows down to the negative pole on the left side, and blasts back up to the positive pole... then shoots into a centrifuge of 10 inch square box as electrical charge for dwelling or office, there is excess, that is sent to power plant and stored for emergency use. We supply the energy to power stations and not the social norm of visa-versa. The charge then flows into the right cylindrical uranium battery and recharges the uranium on right side, then the blast hits bottom of negative pole, blasts back up thru positive pole and into centrifuge, sends electricity into dwelling and excess is sent to power generators globally. Blast returns into left battery cylinder and, recharges uranium isotopes of low grain power and the cycle continues for entire "recharged" uranium half-life. There is no fear of uranium leakage, and should have standby switch when not using and emergency shut off for electrical wiring repair due to storms, faulty installment damage.

DAVID M PEDJOE
http://www.onemodelplace.com/artists/apsi-mesti,

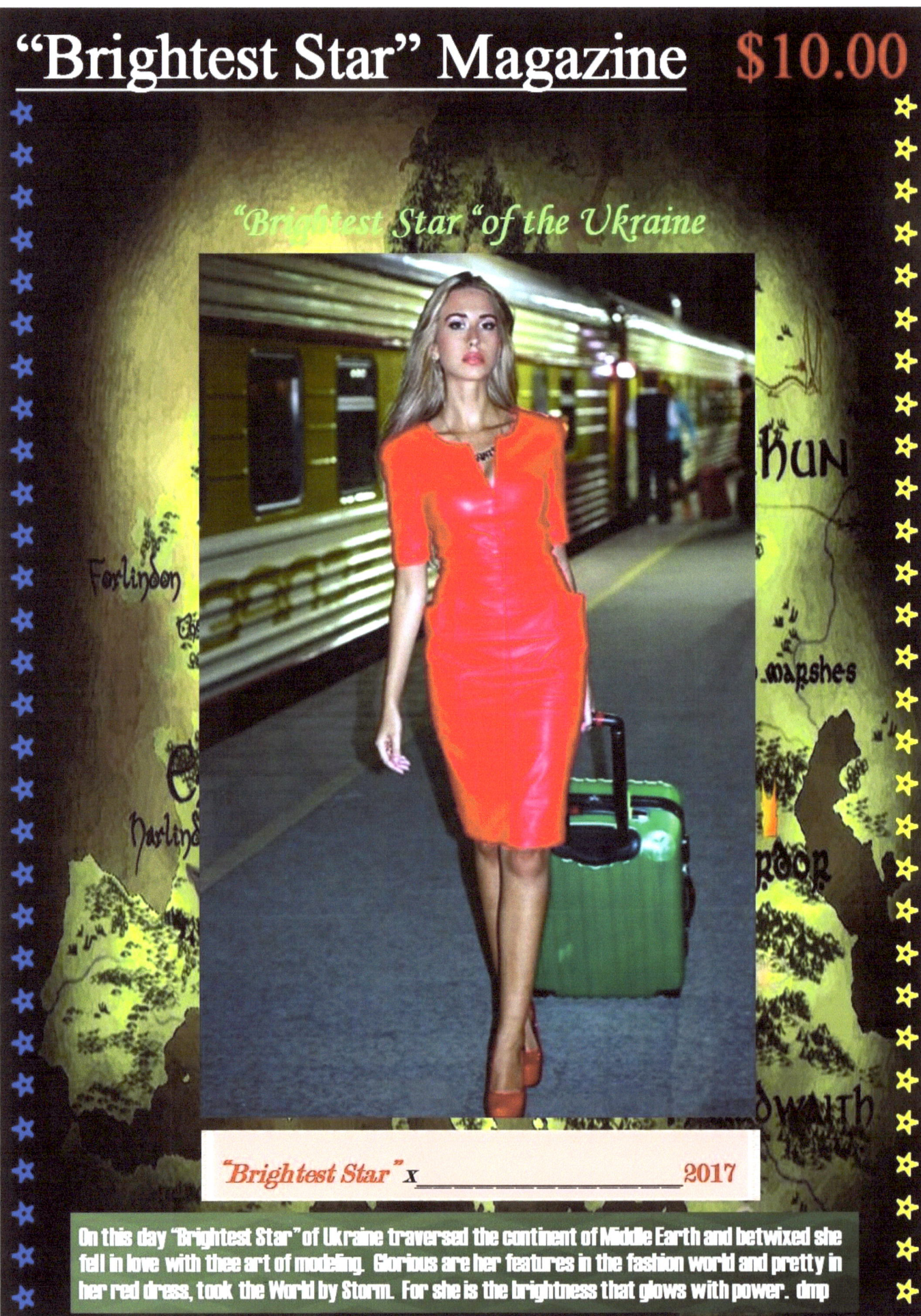

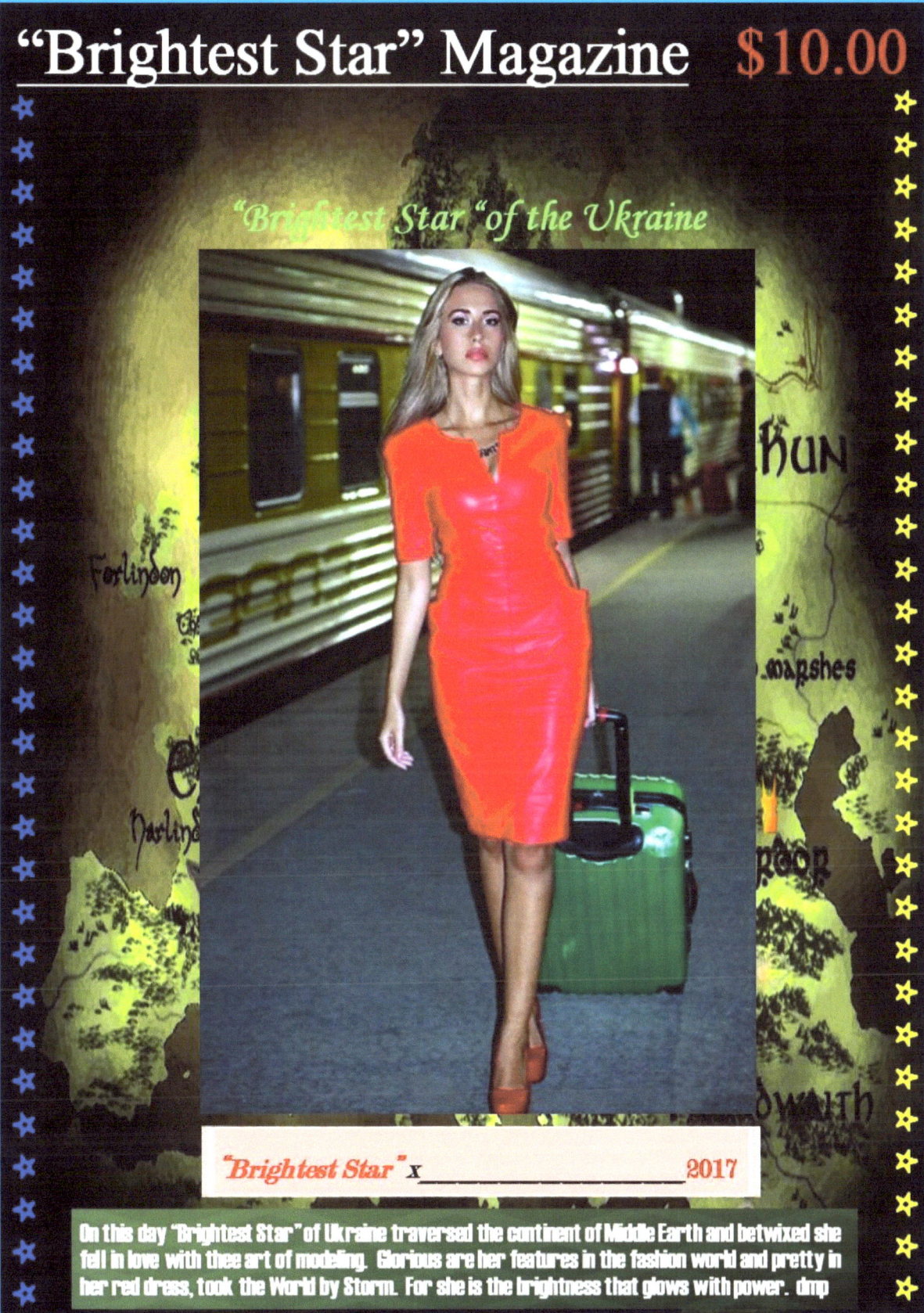

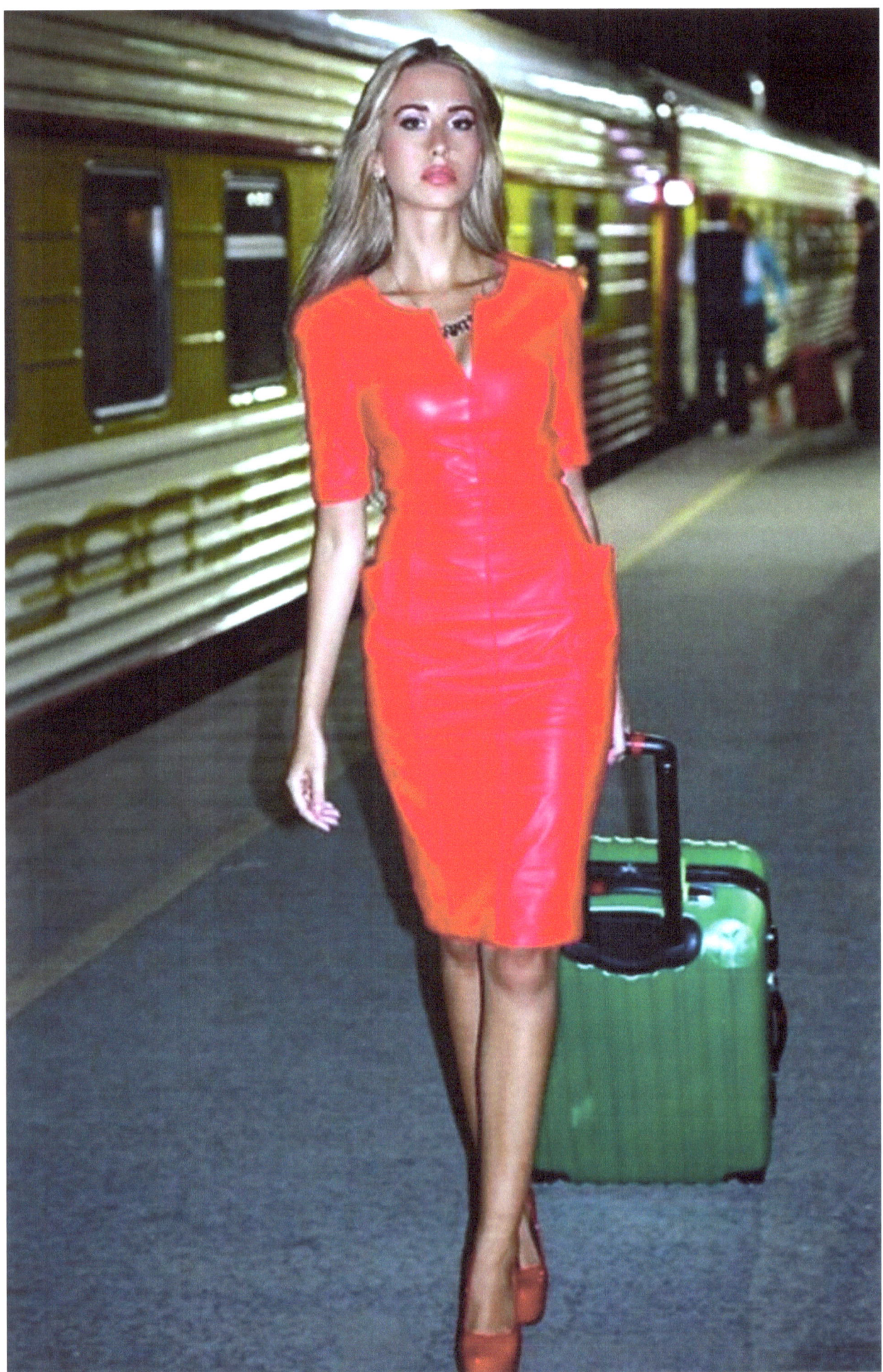

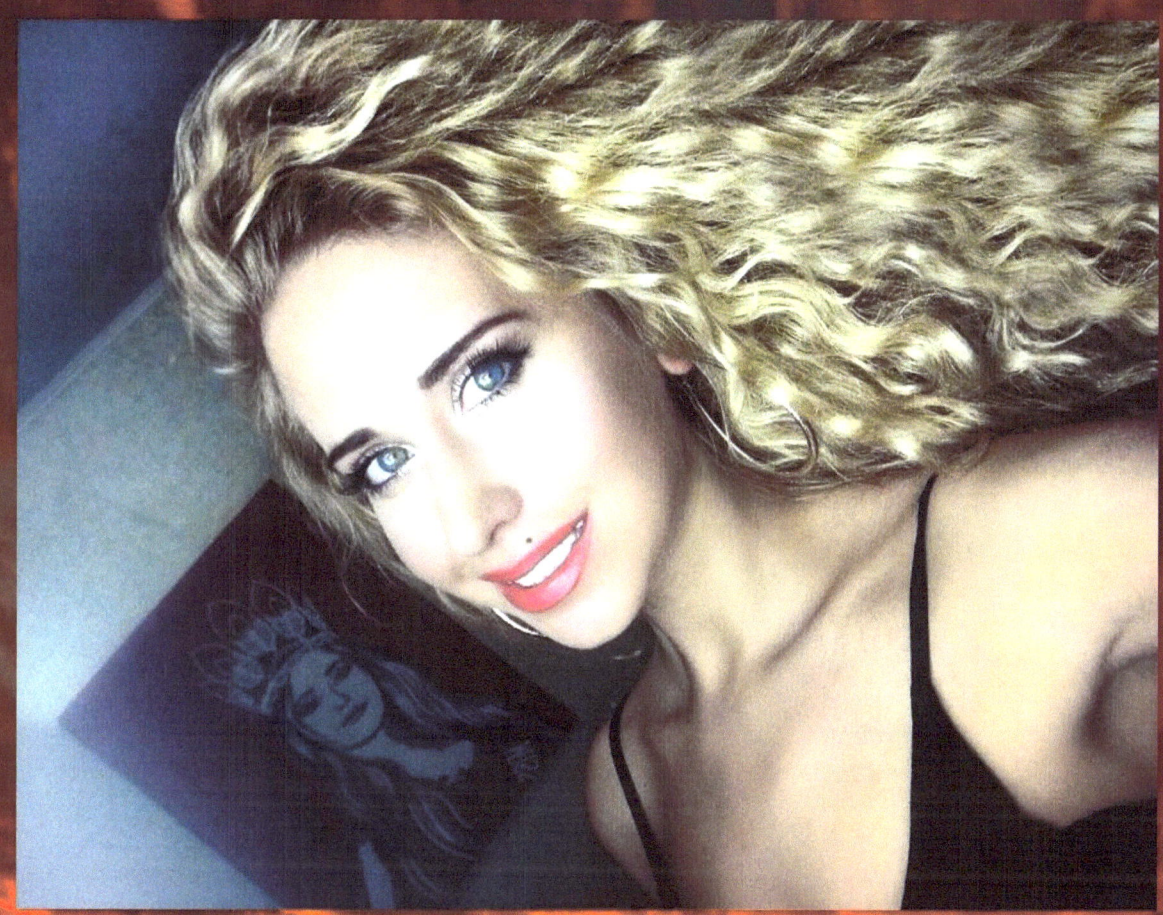

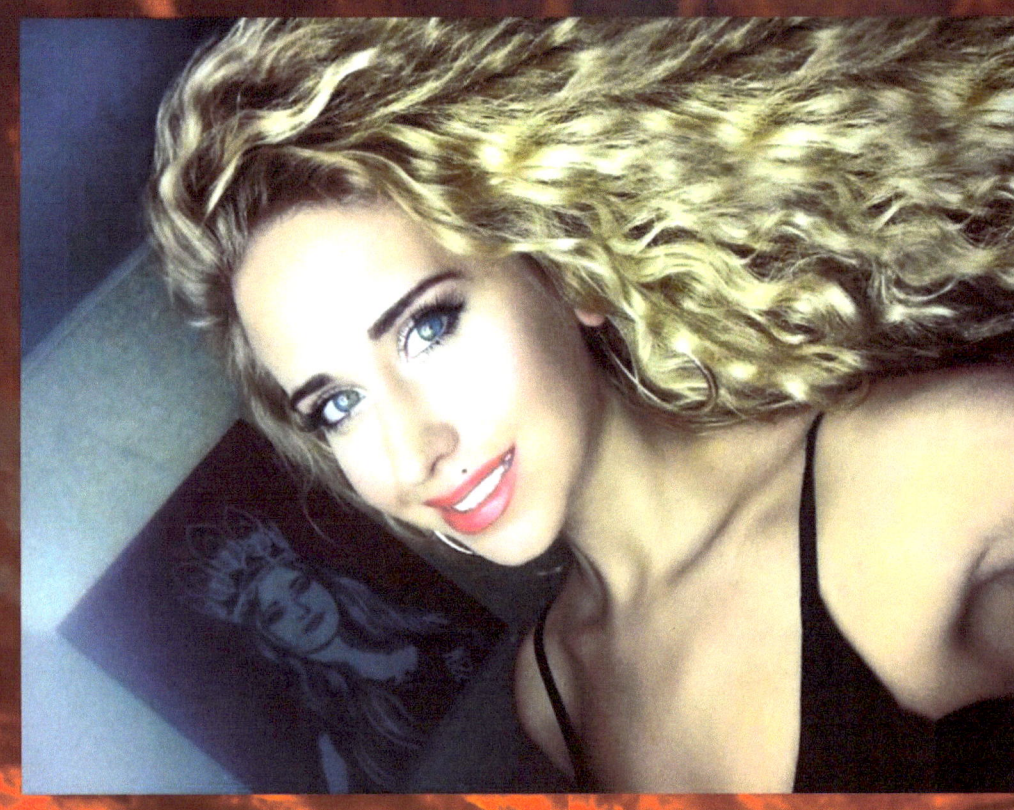

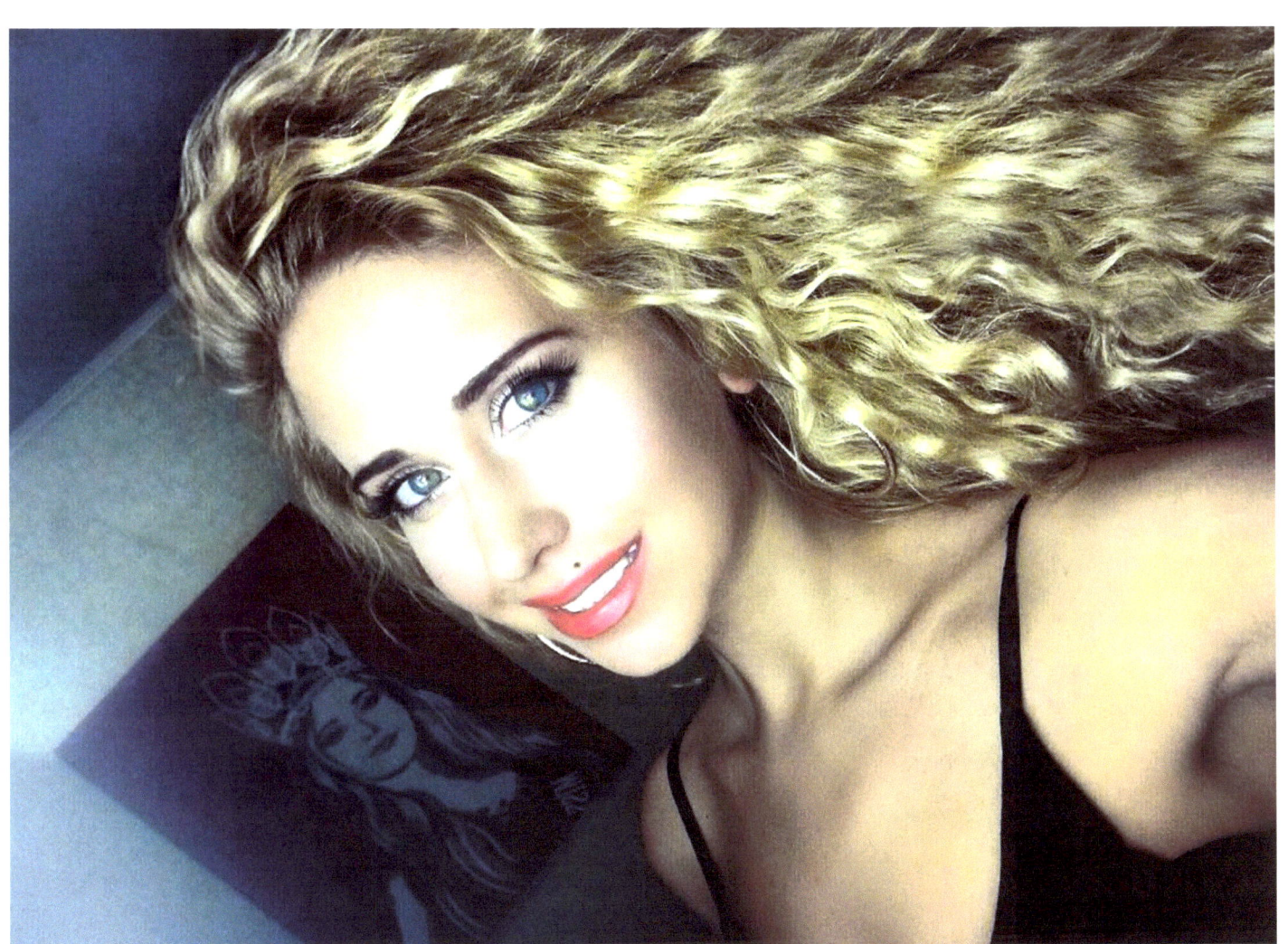

"Brightest Star" Magazine $10.00
===

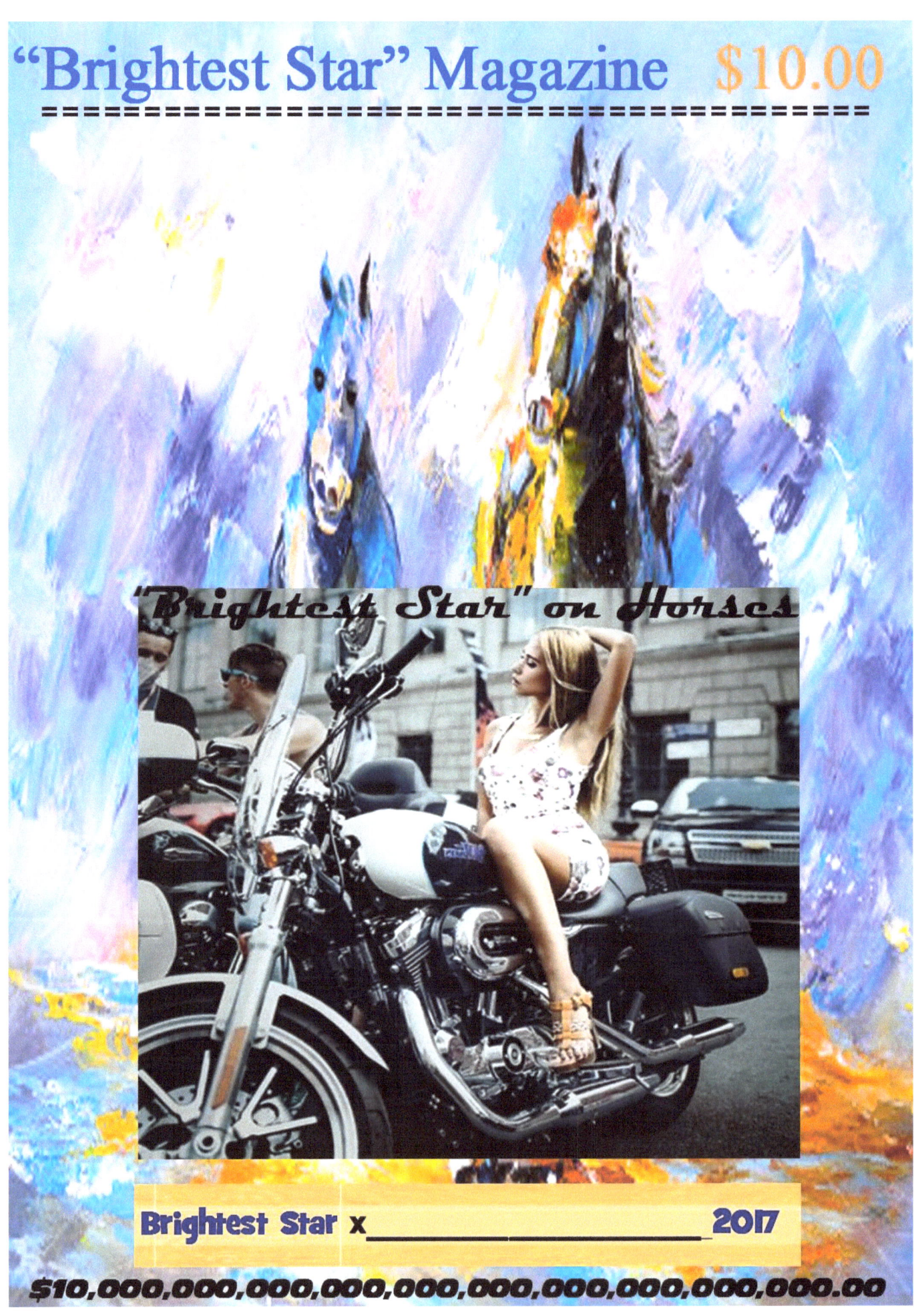

"Brightest Star" on Horses

Brightest Star x_____ 2017

$10,000,000,000,000,000,000,000,000,000,000.00

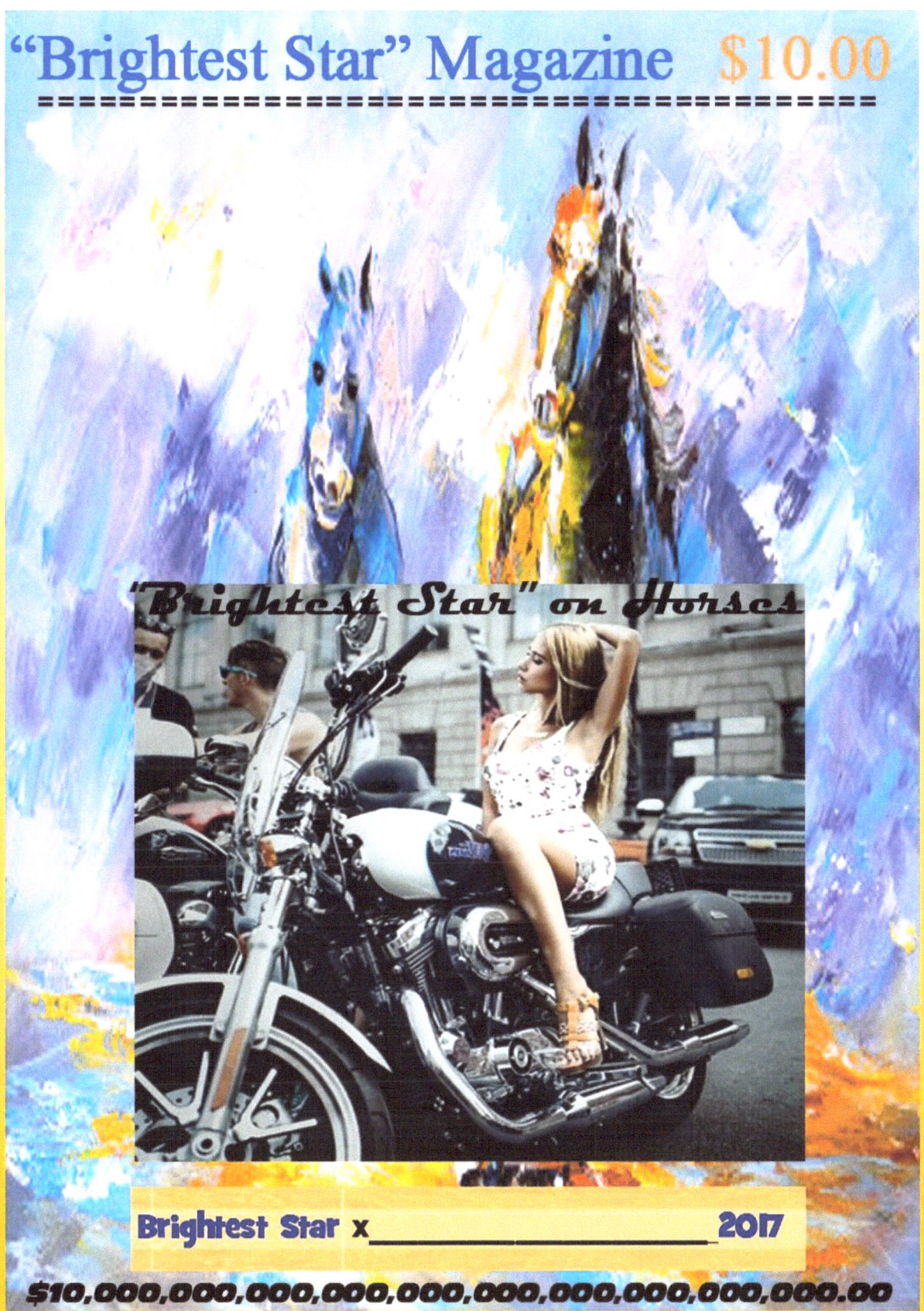

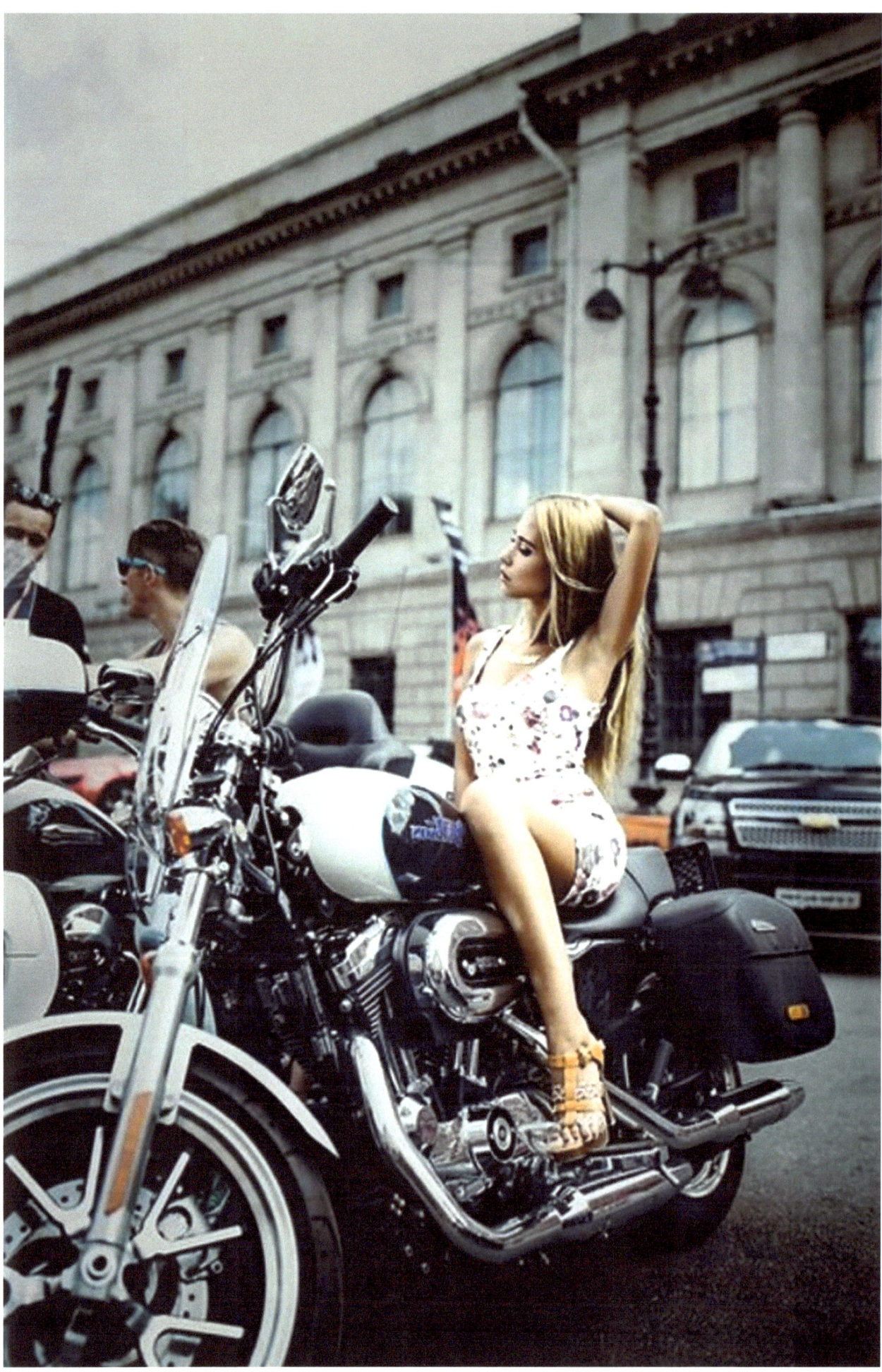

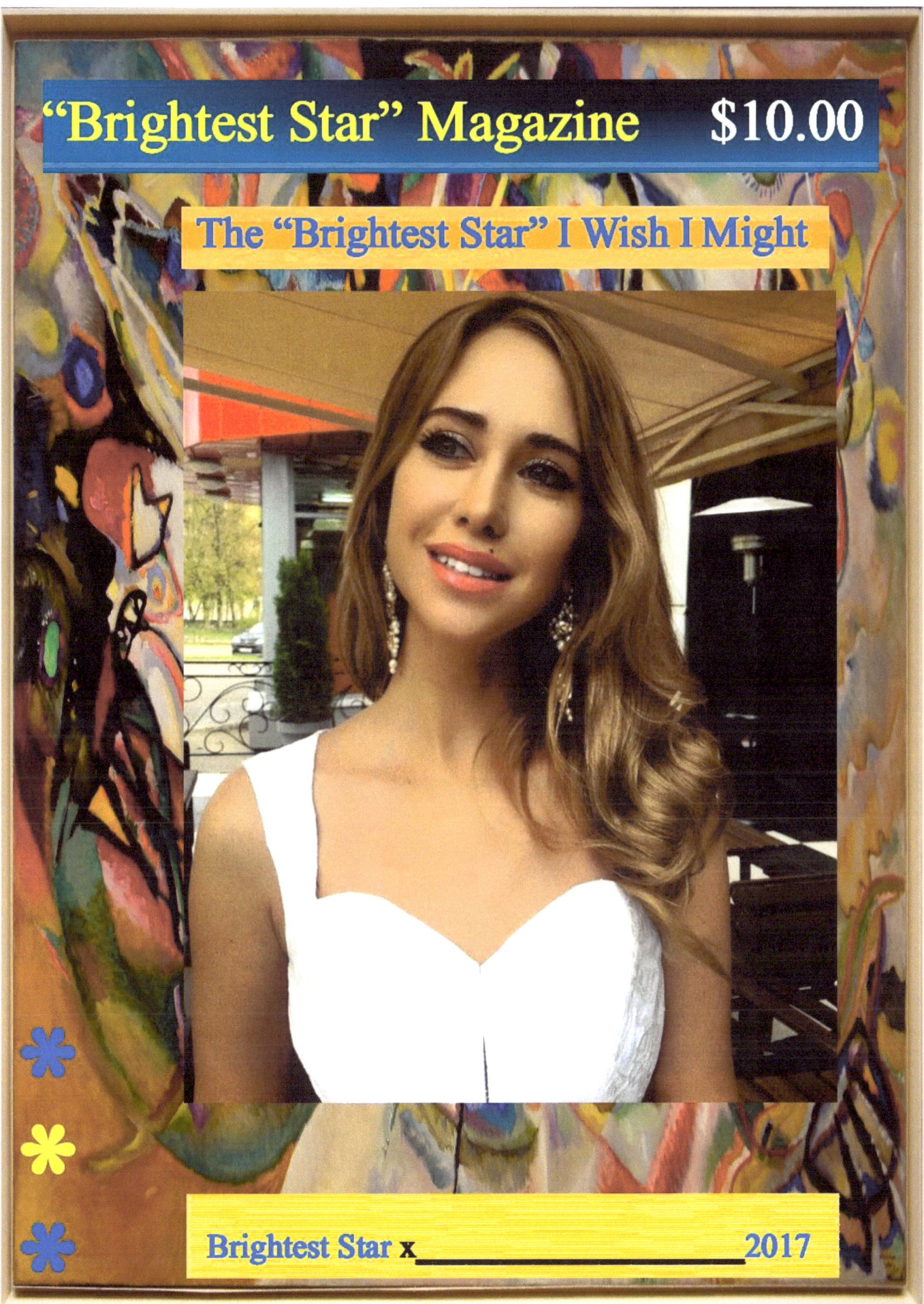

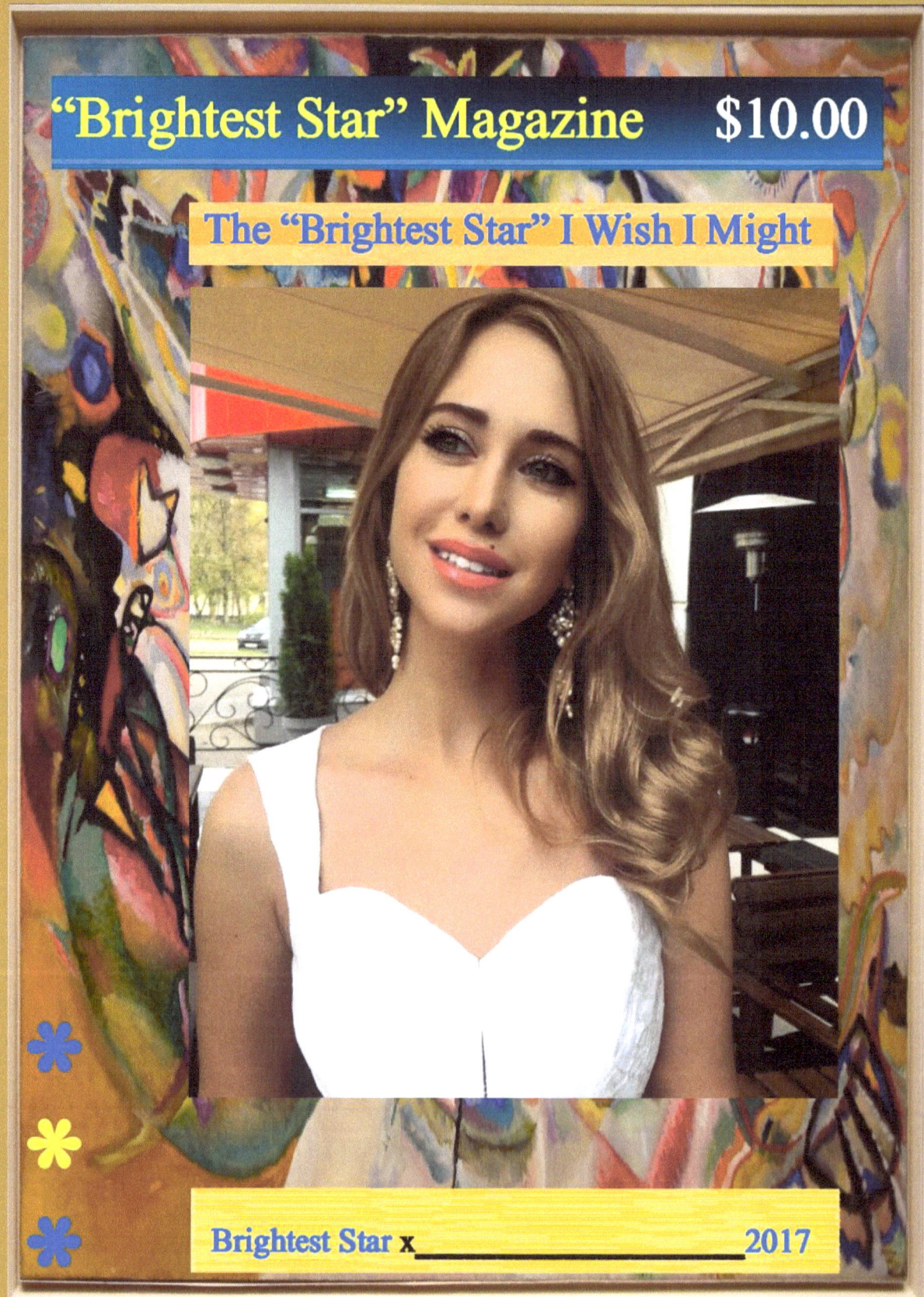

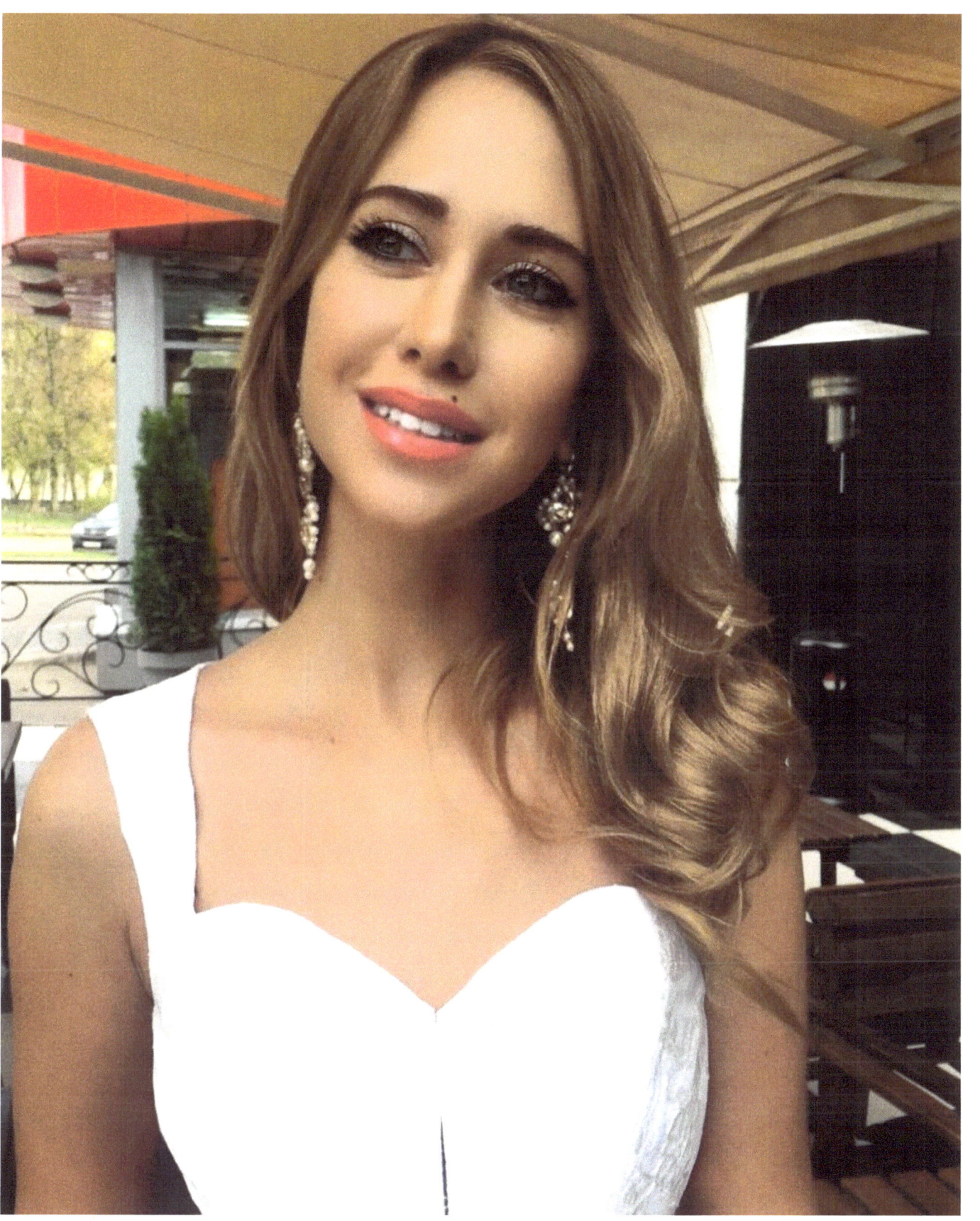

★★★★★ ★ ★★★★★
"BRiGHTEST STAR" MAGAZiNE $10

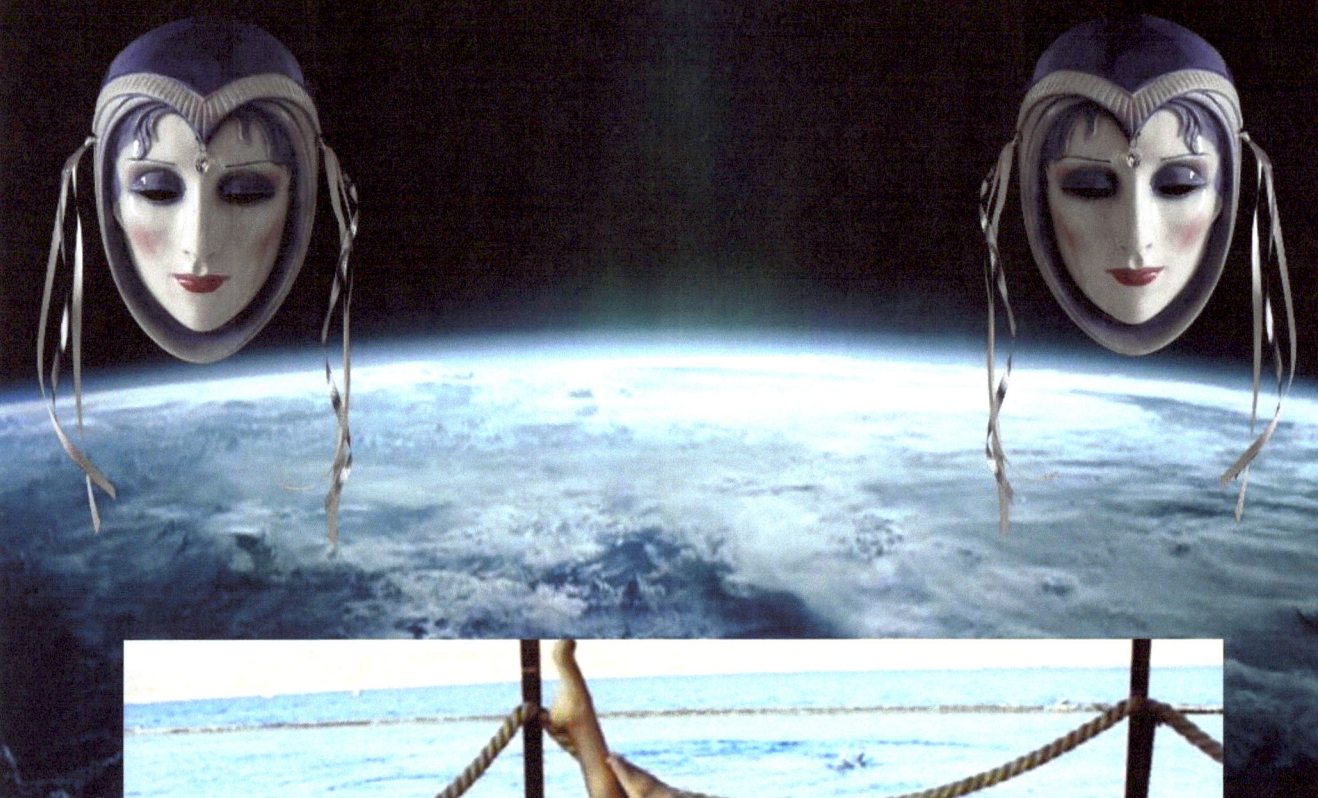

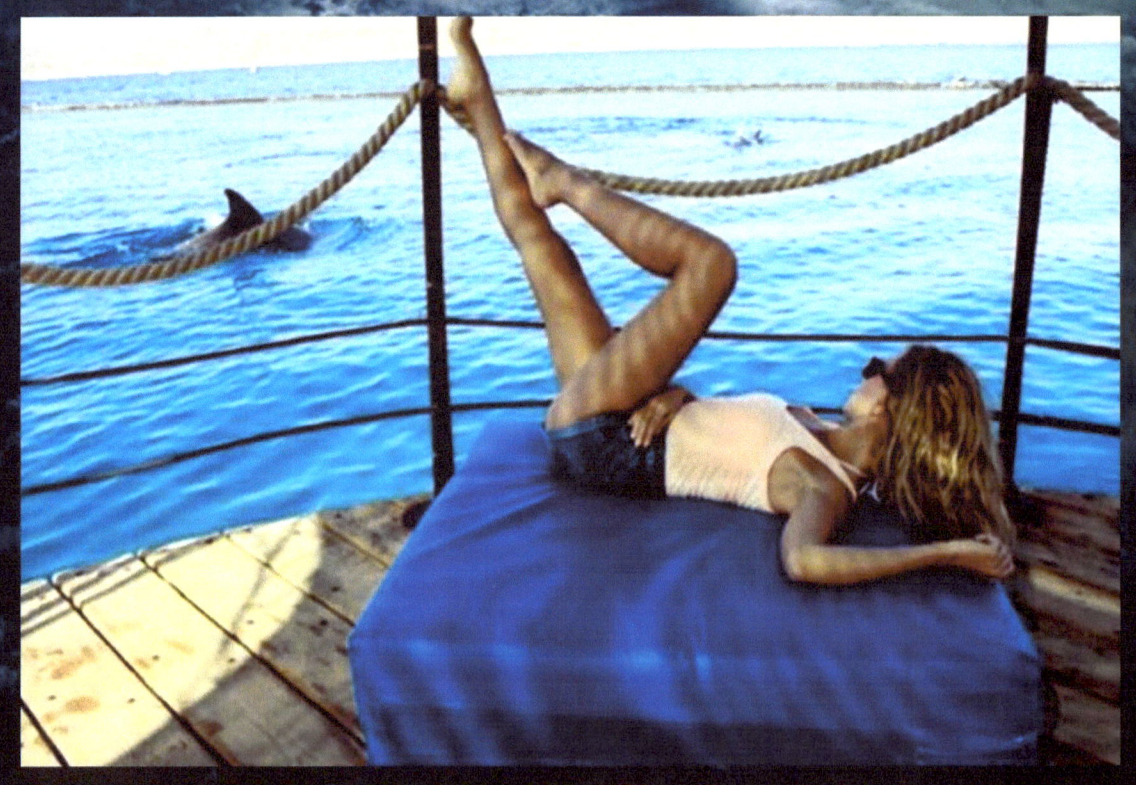

 "Brightest Star" x_____ 2017

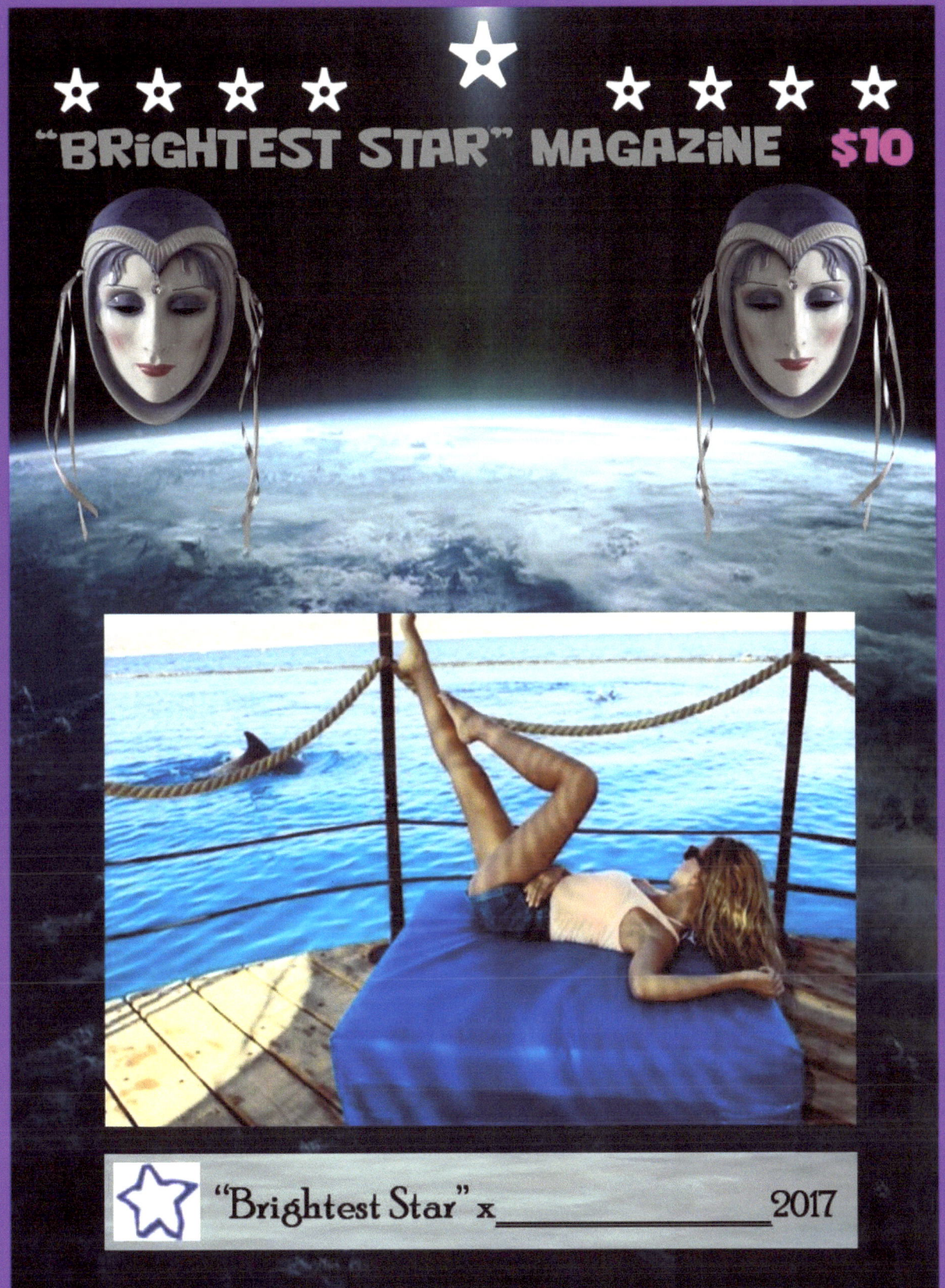

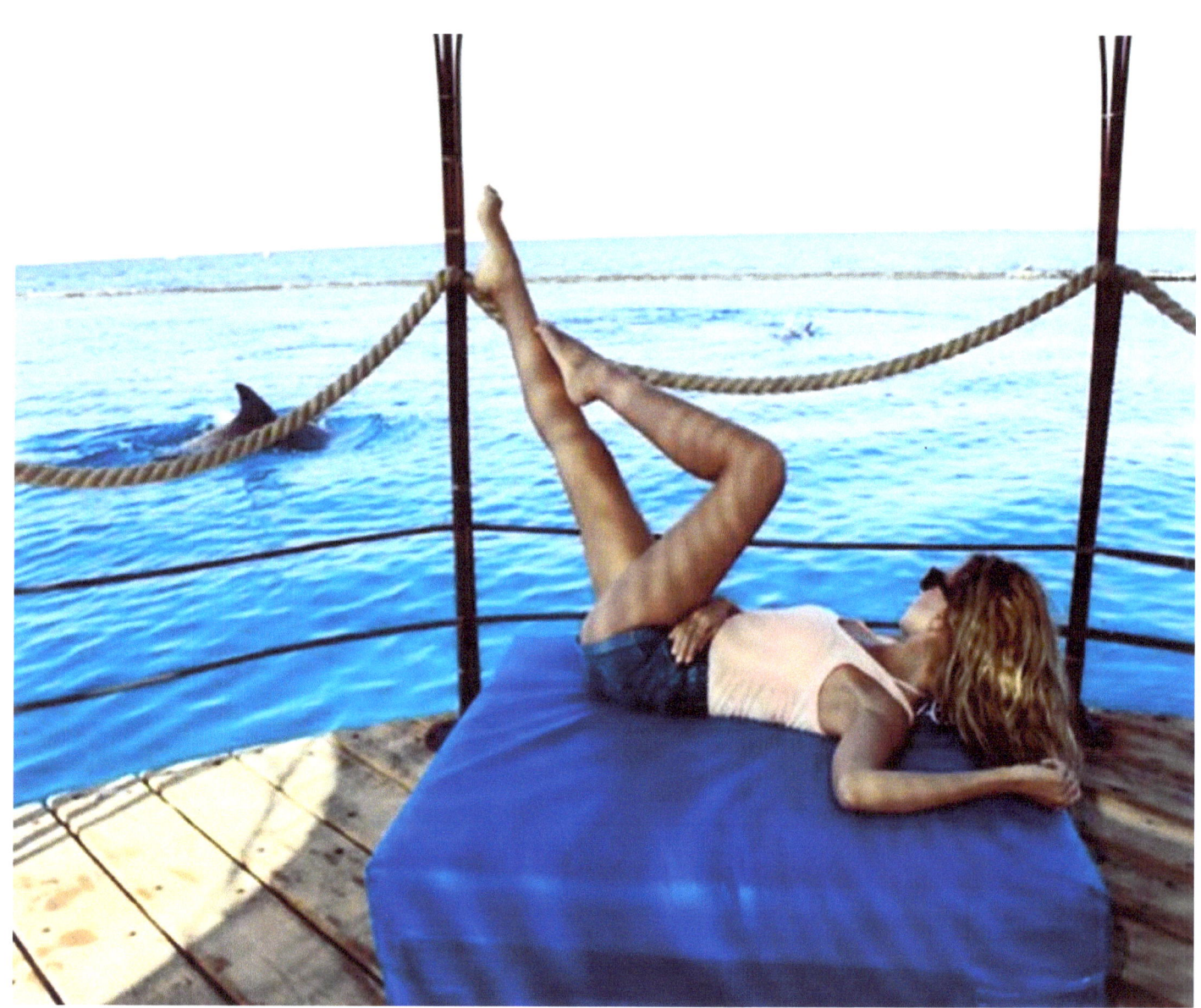

"Brightest Star" Magazine $10

"Brightest Star" captivating the Lion

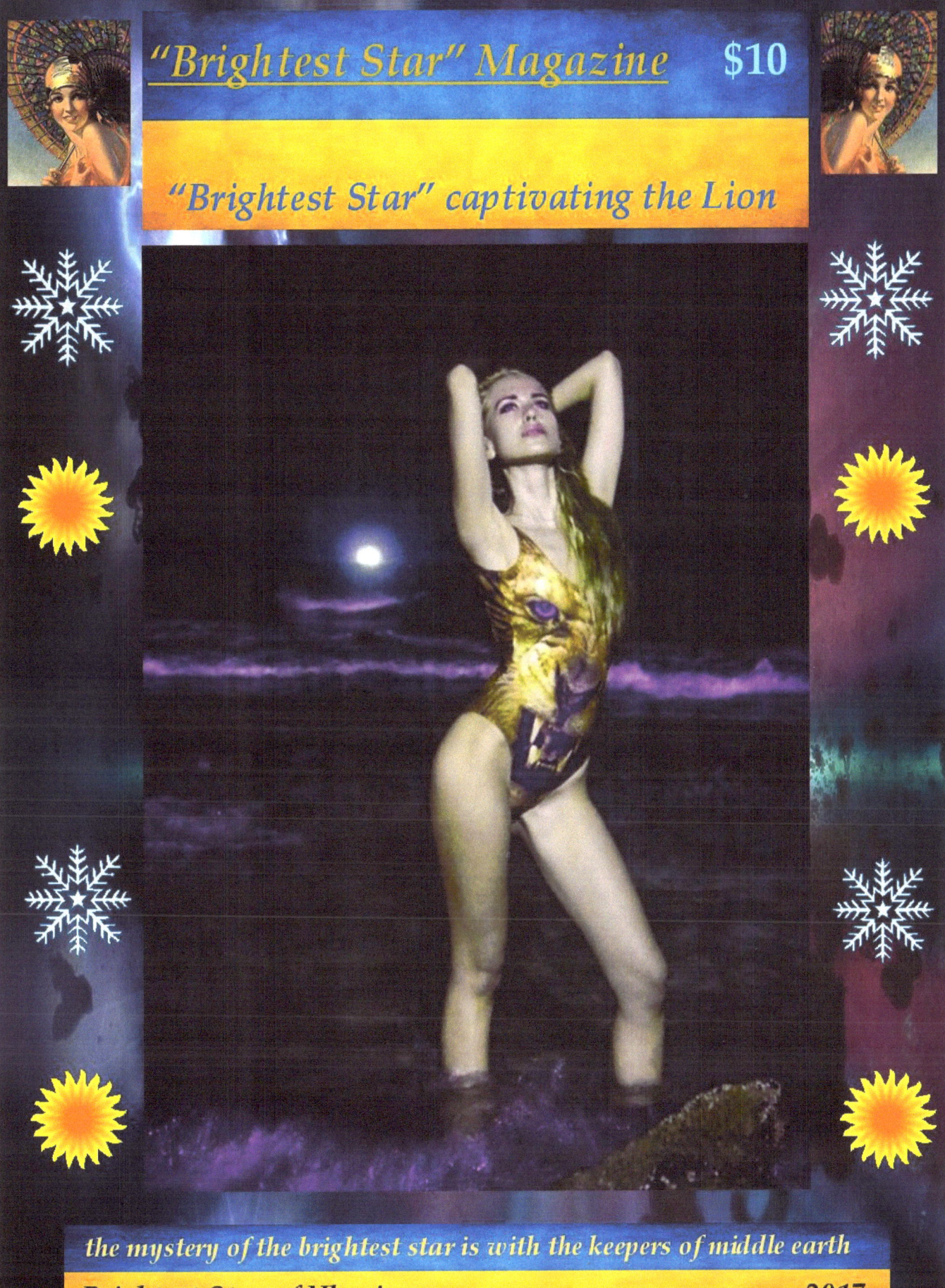

the mystery of the brightest star is with the keepers of middle earth

Brightest Star of Ukraine x _____ 2017

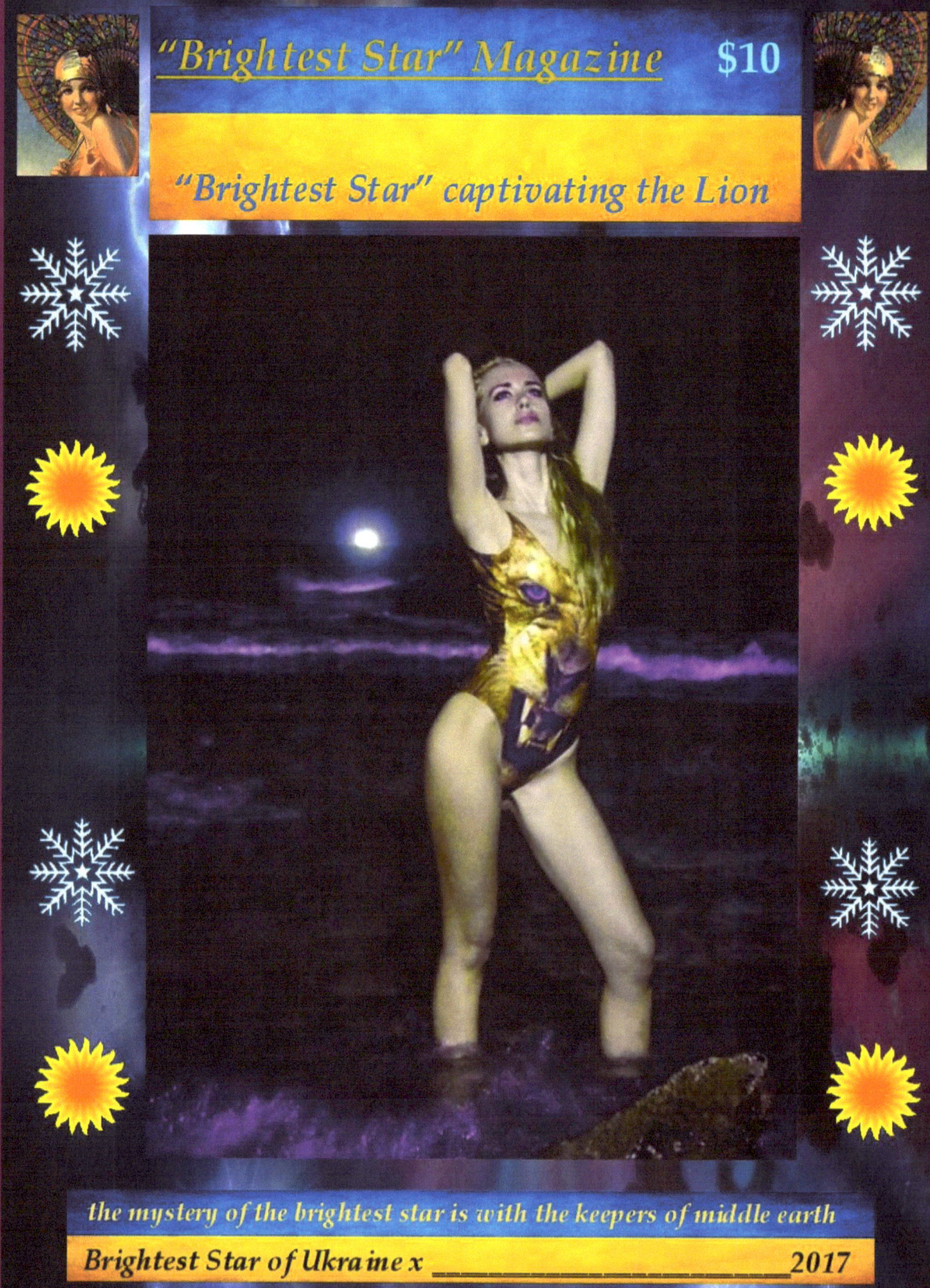

"Brightest Star" Magazine $10

"Brightest Star" captivating the Lion

the mystery of the brightest star is with the keepers of middle earth

Brightest Star of Ukraine x_____ 2017

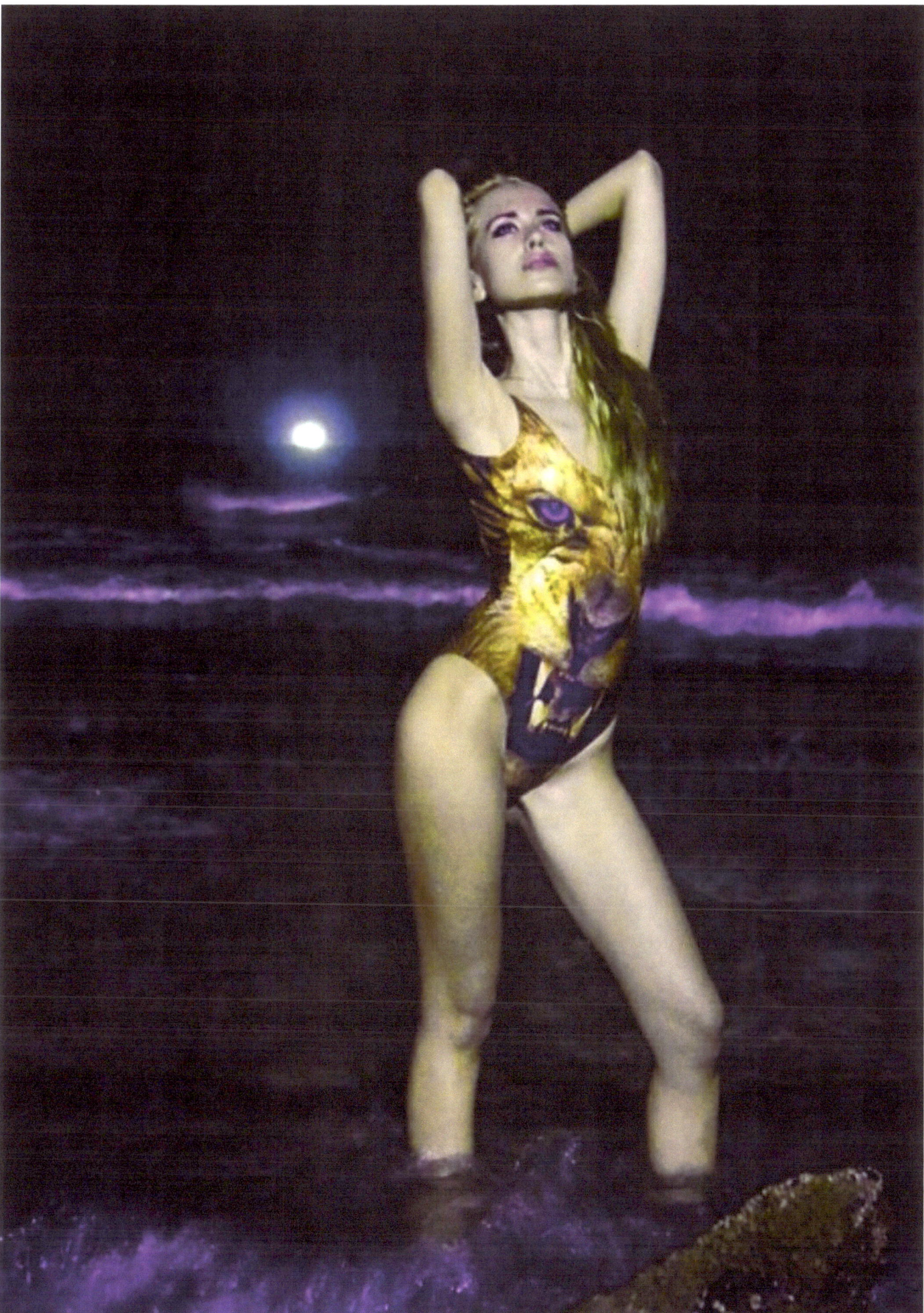

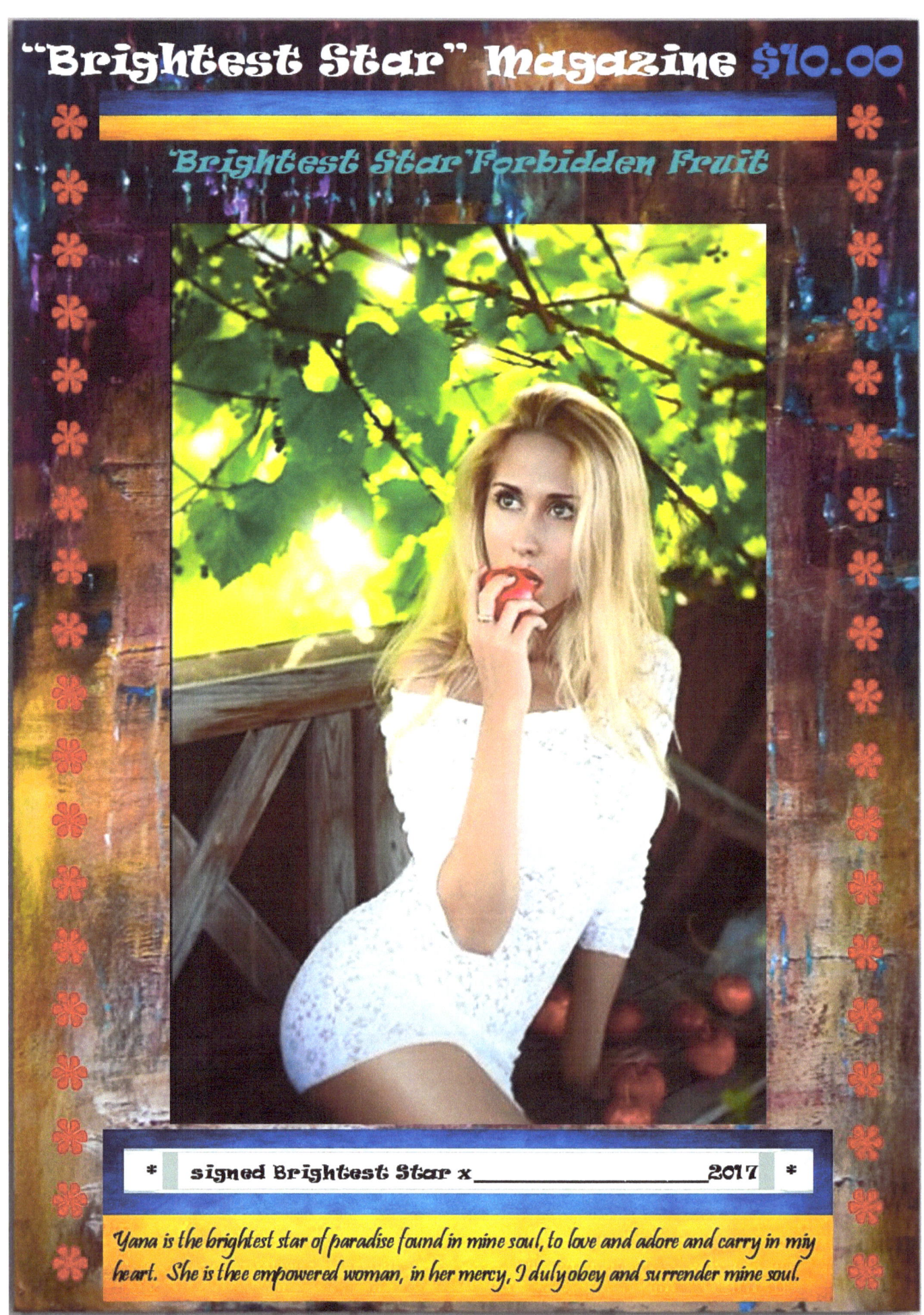

"Brightest Star" Magazine $10.00

"Brightest Star" Forbidden Fruit

* signed Brightest Star x_____2017 *

Yana is the brightest star of paradise found in mine soul, to love and adore and carry in my heart. She is thee empowered woman, in her mercy, I duly obey and surrender mine soul.

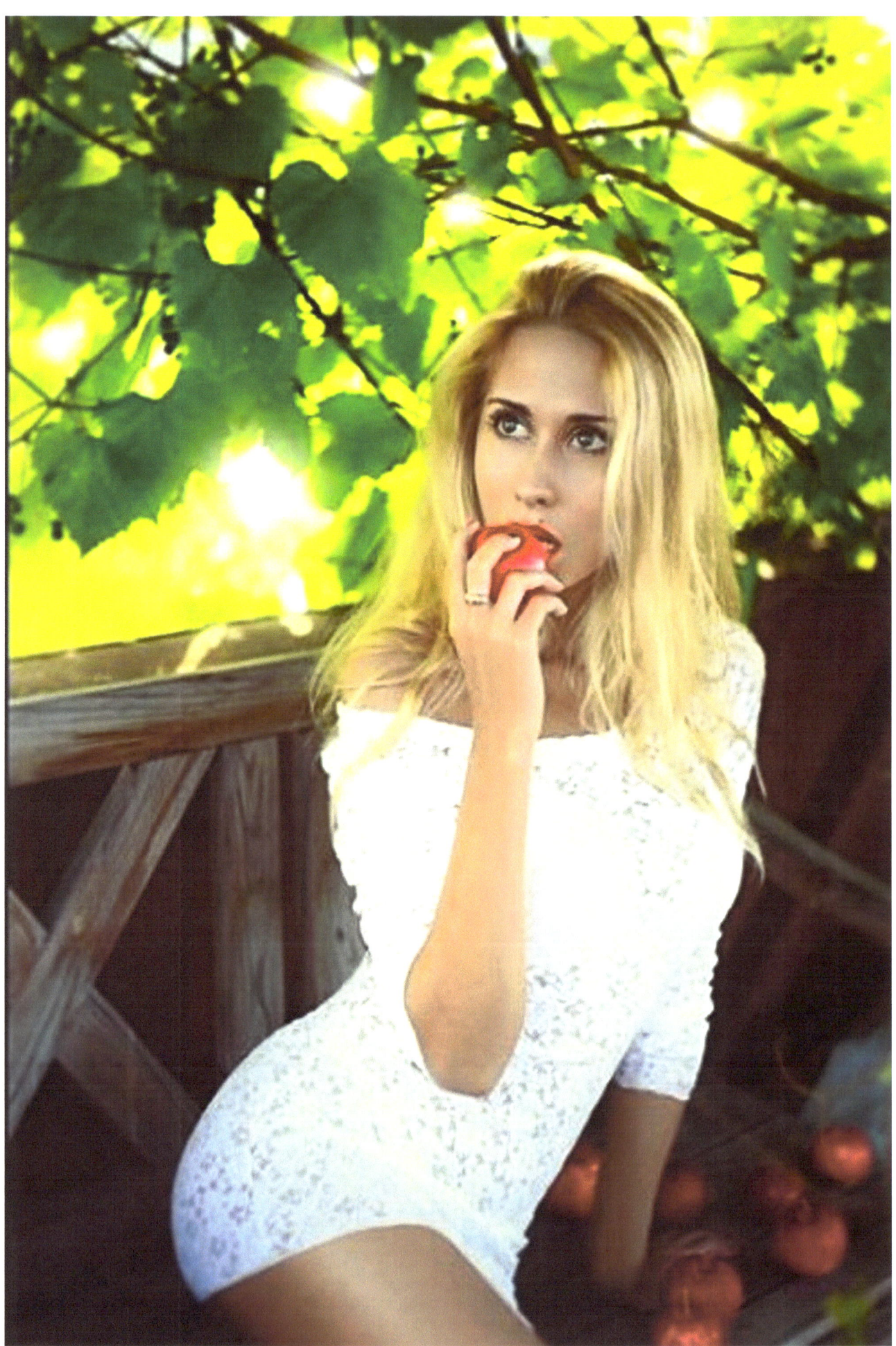

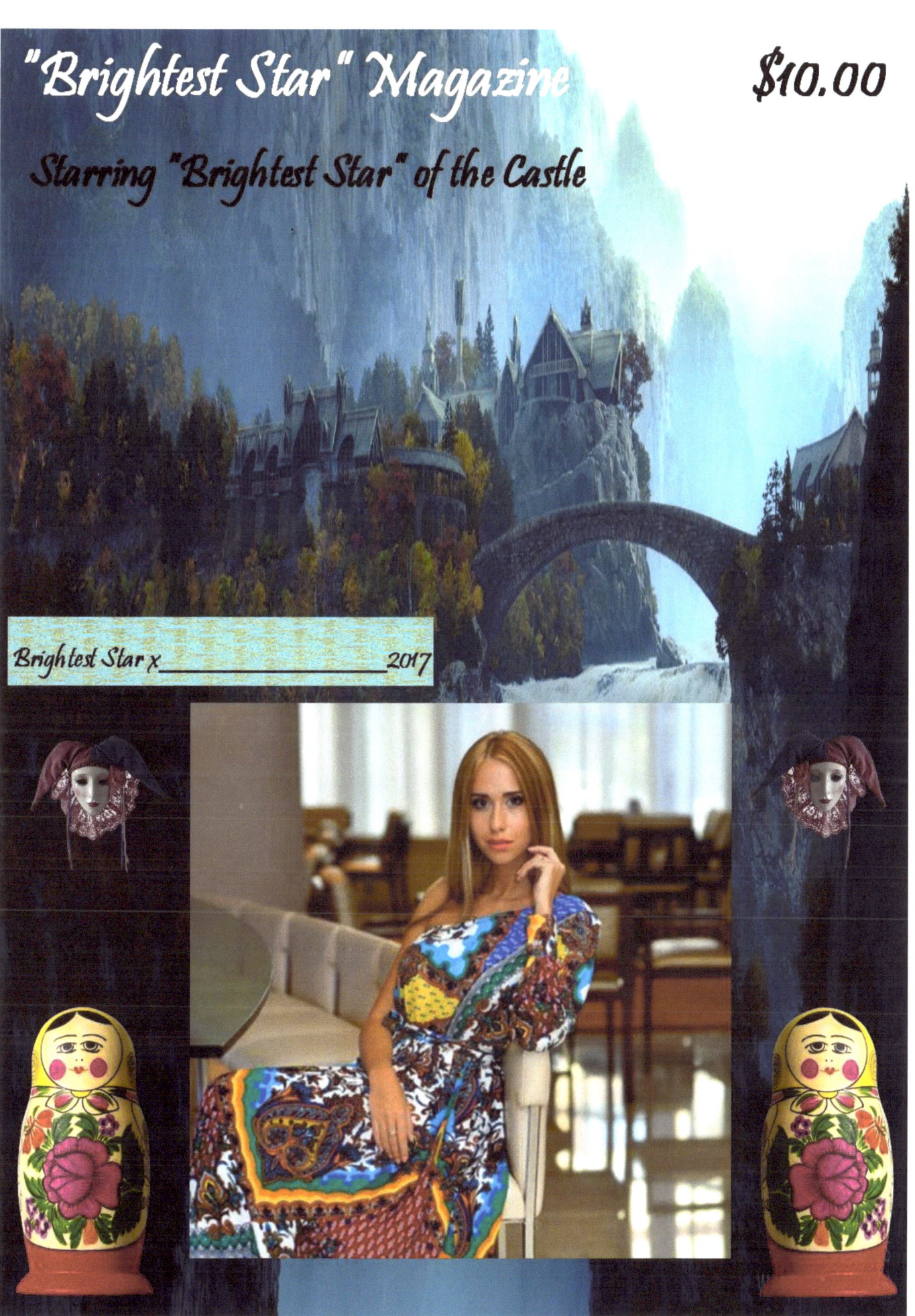

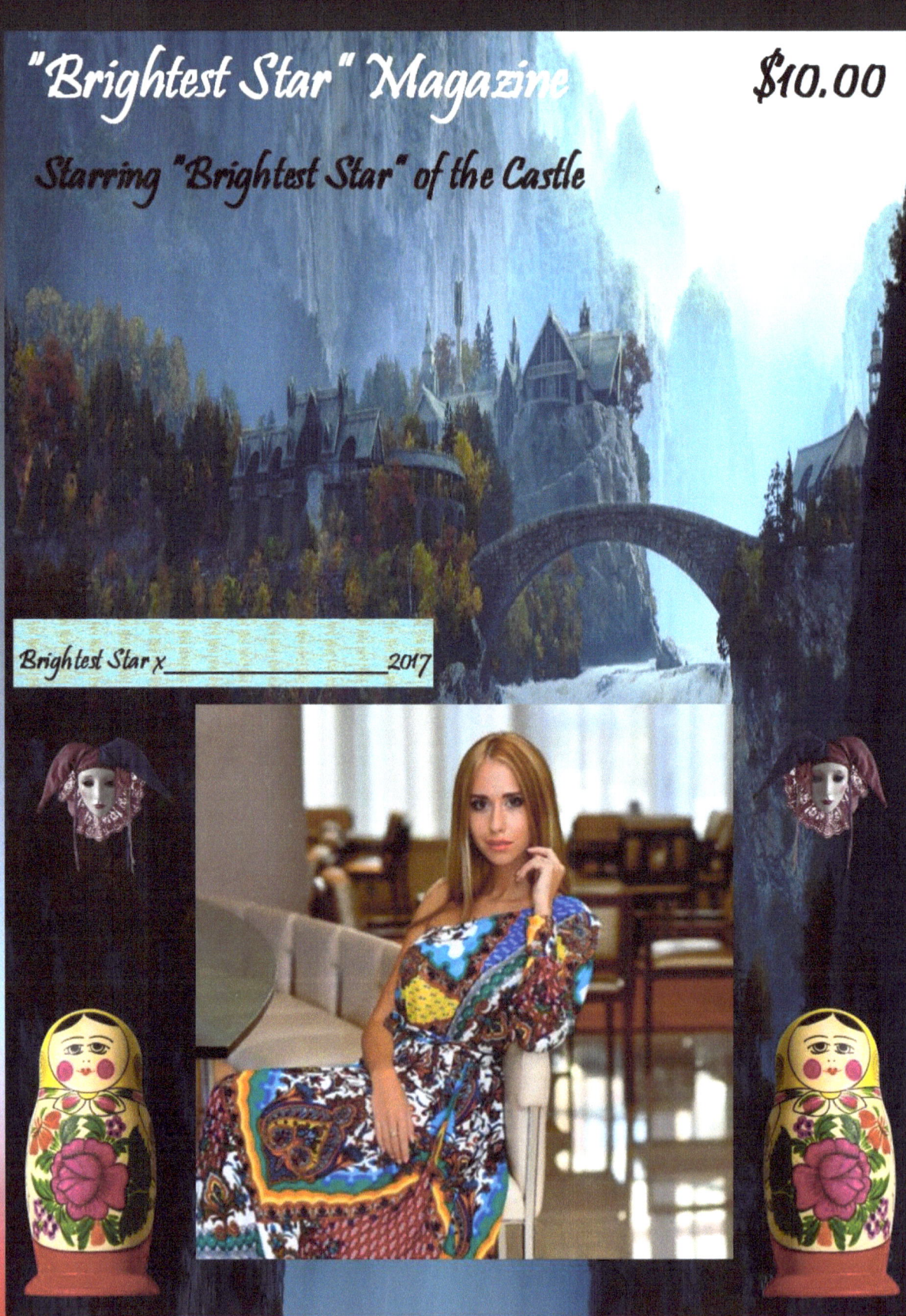

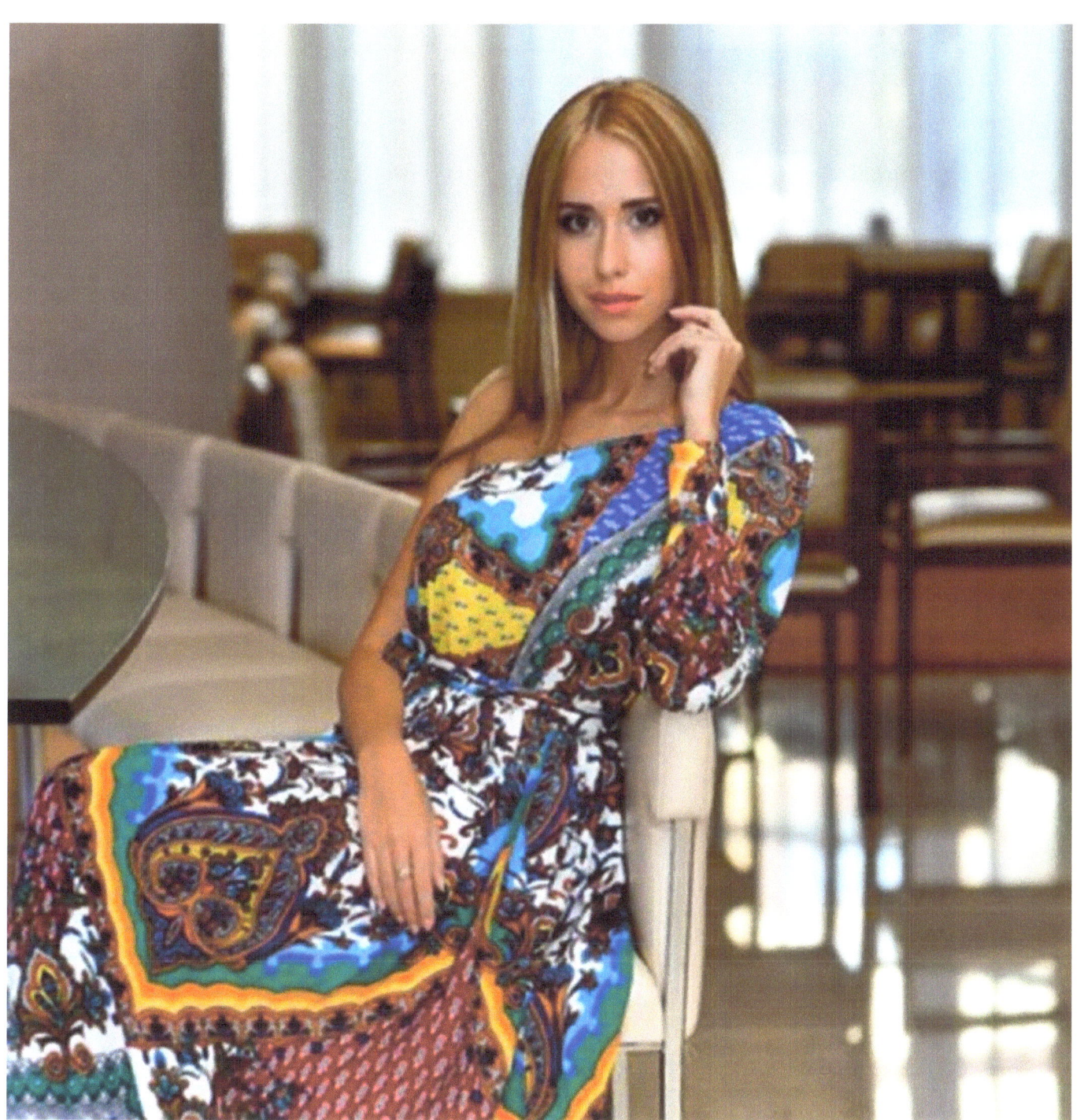

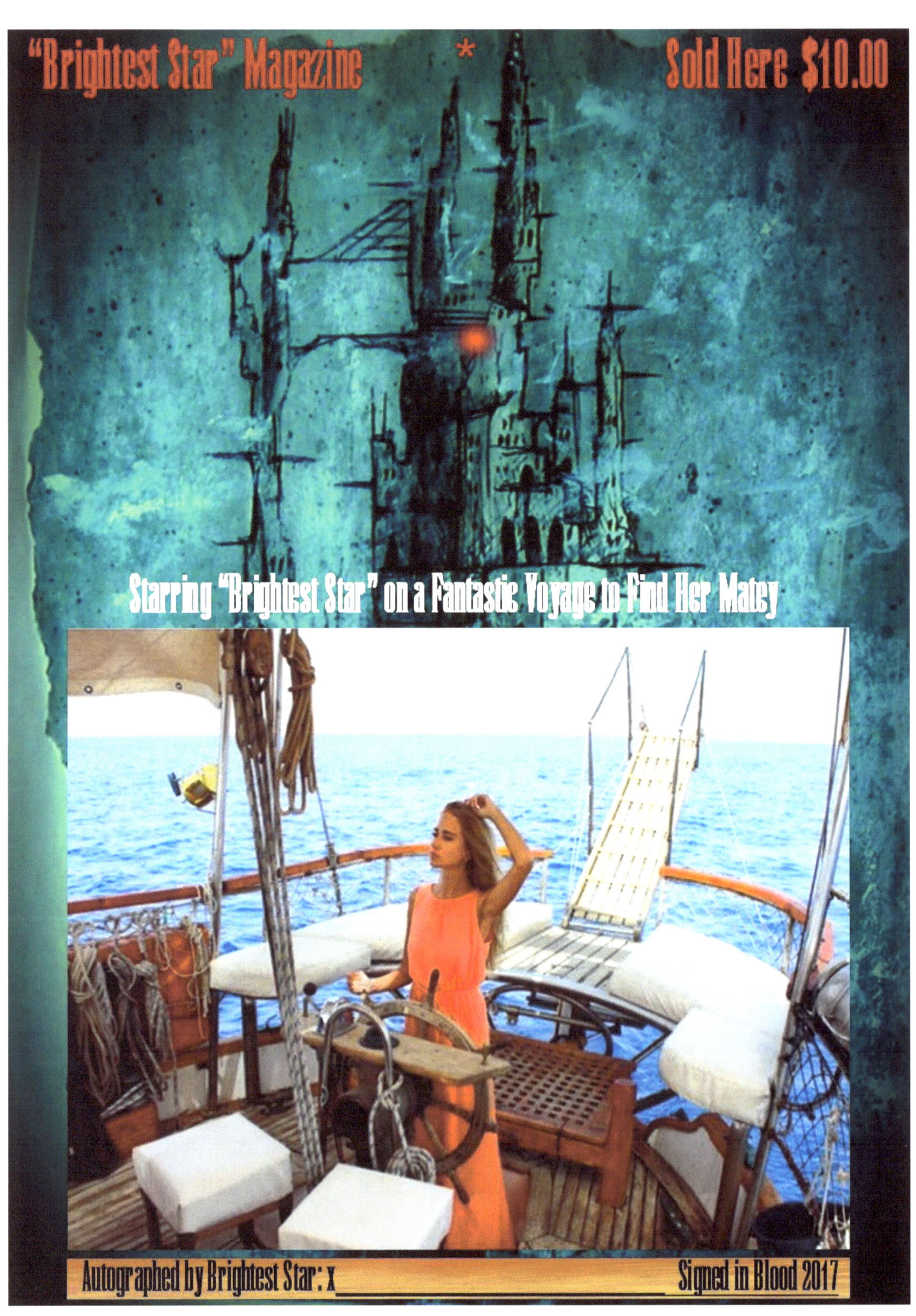

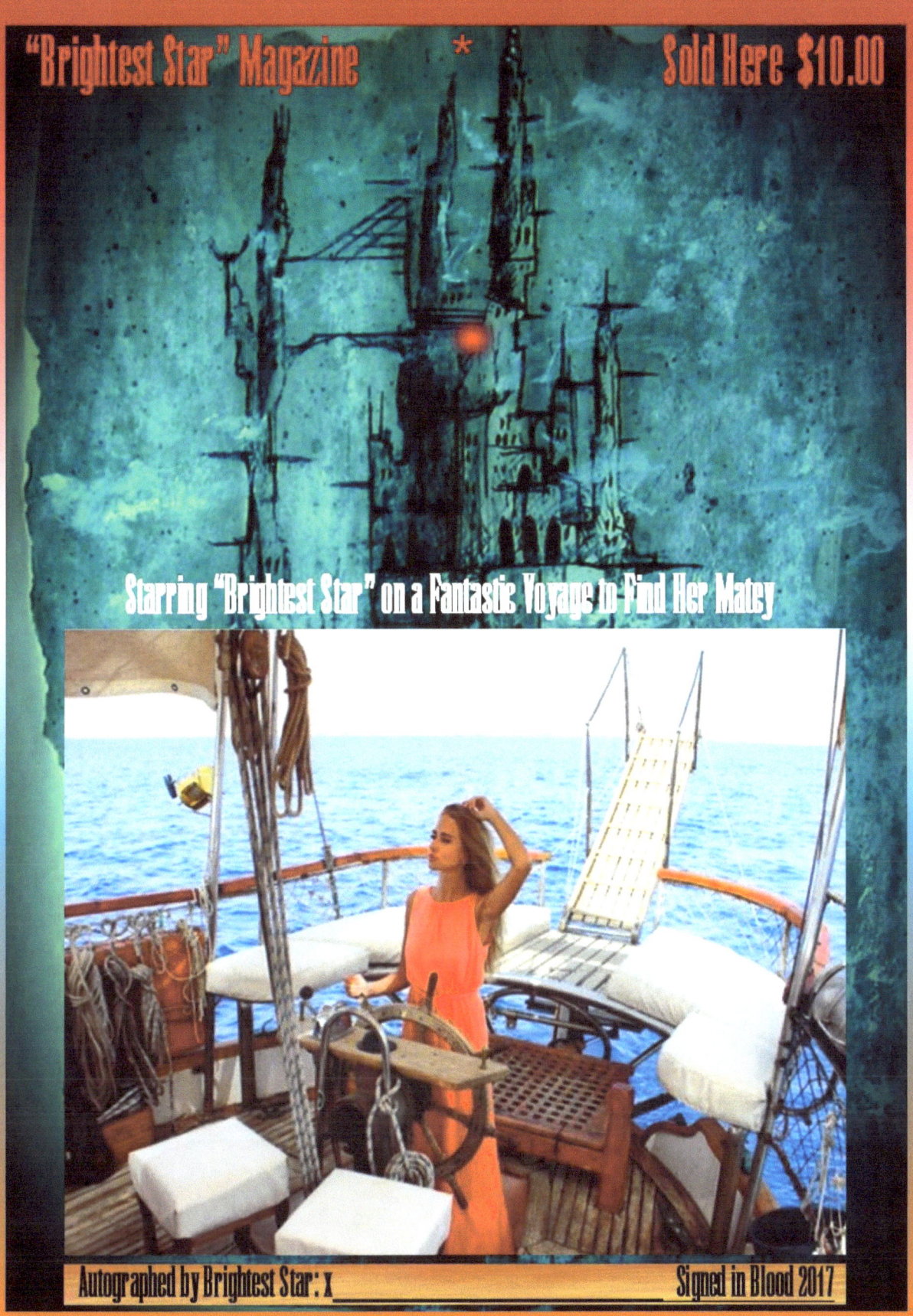

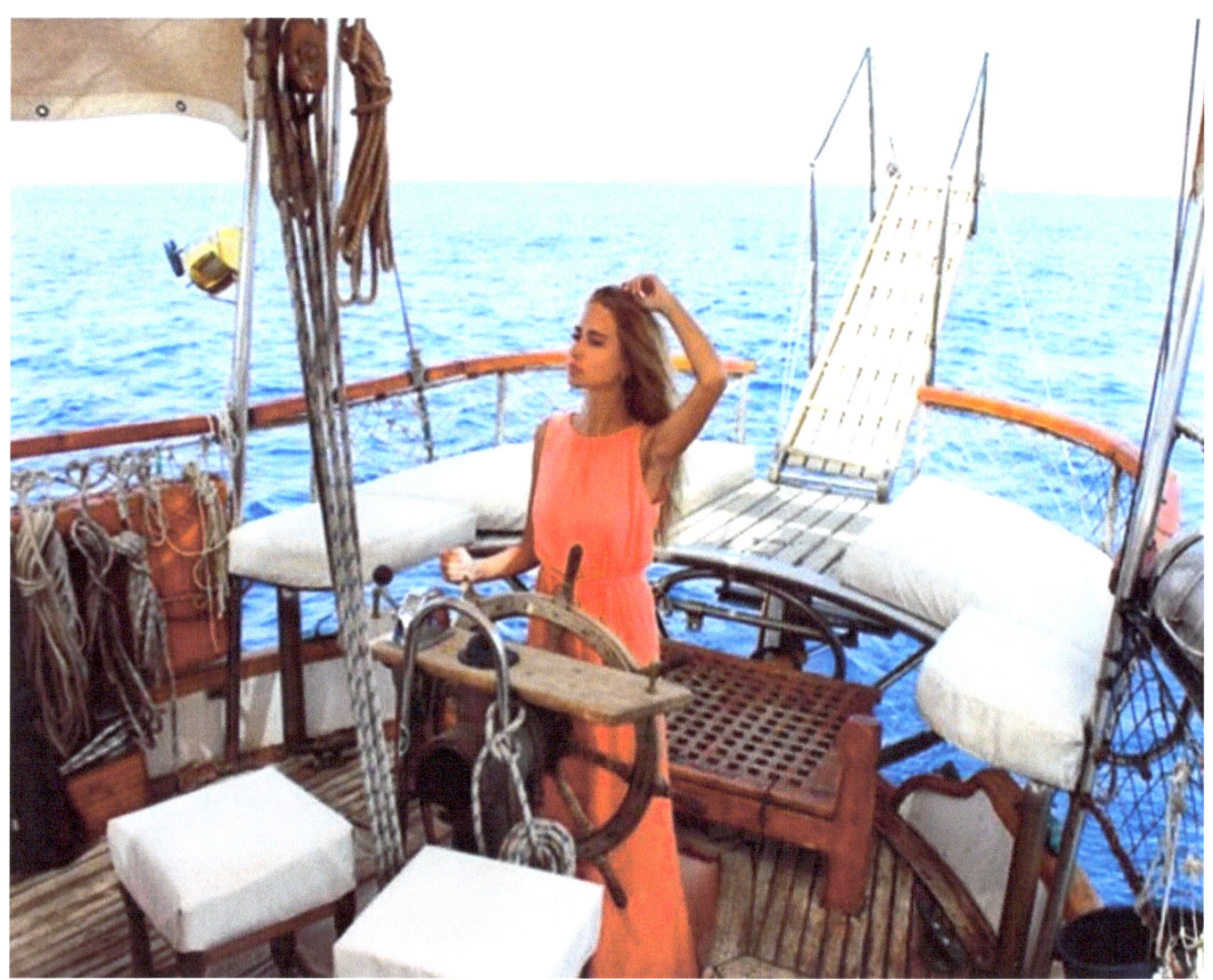

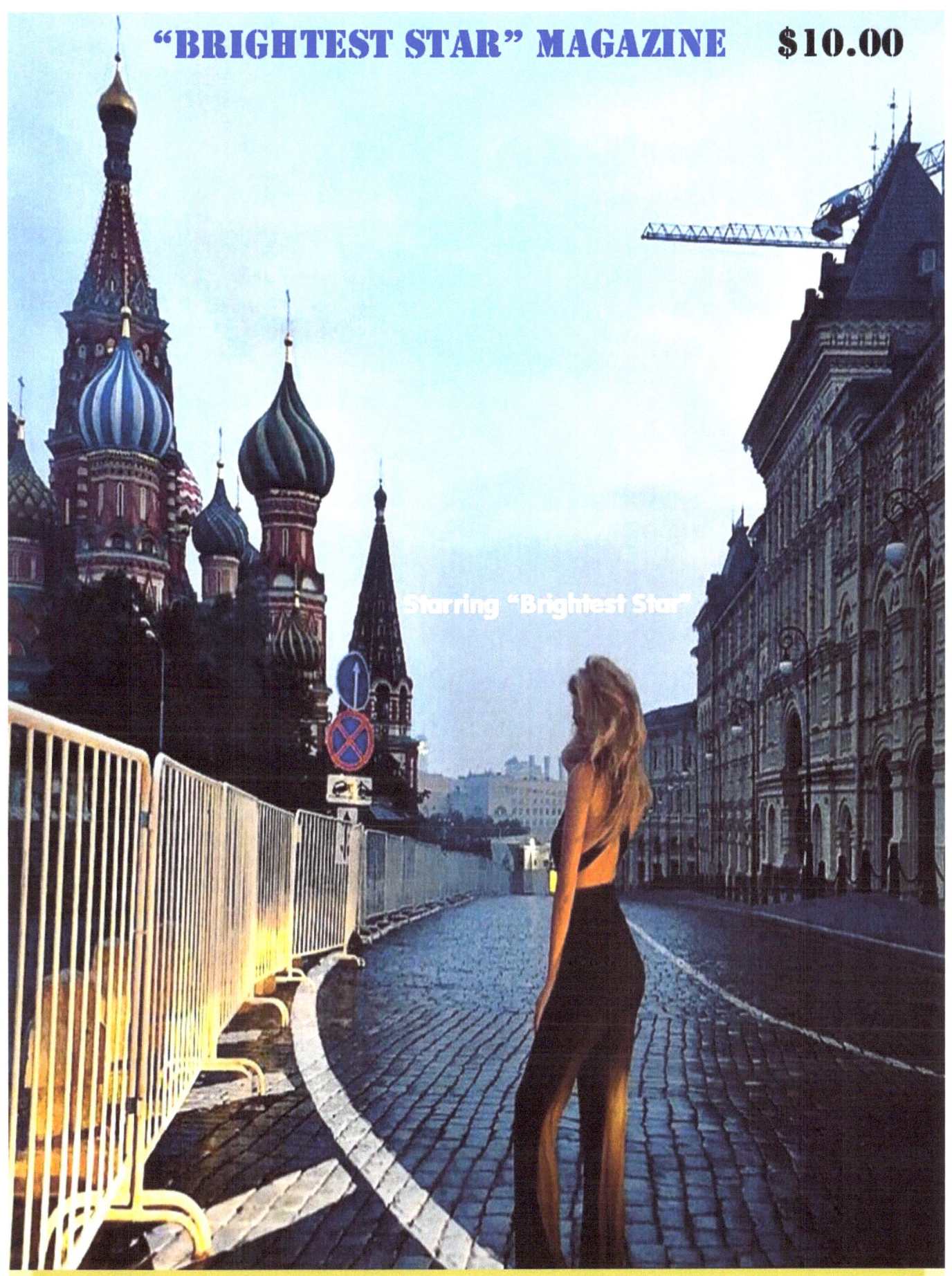

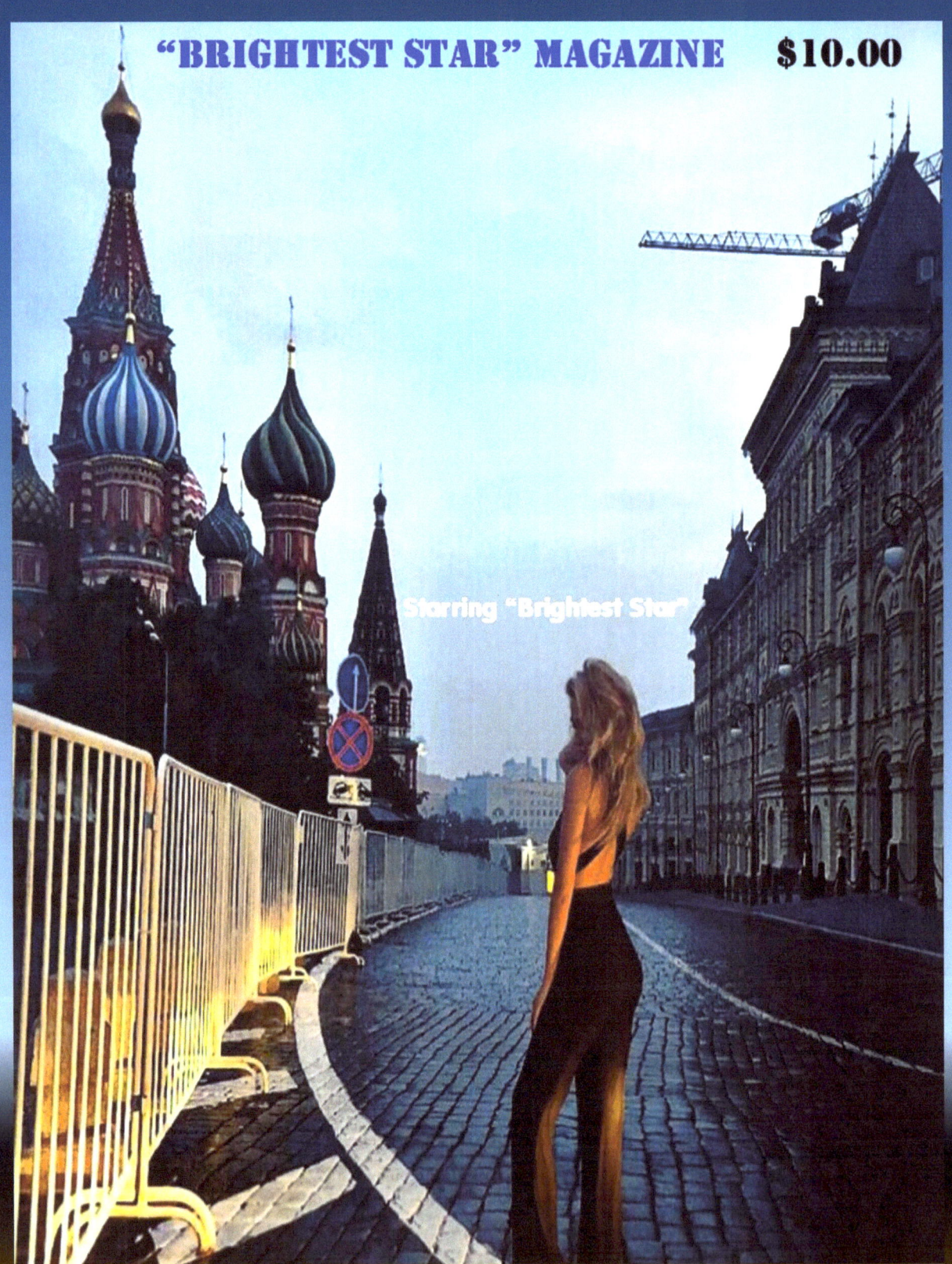

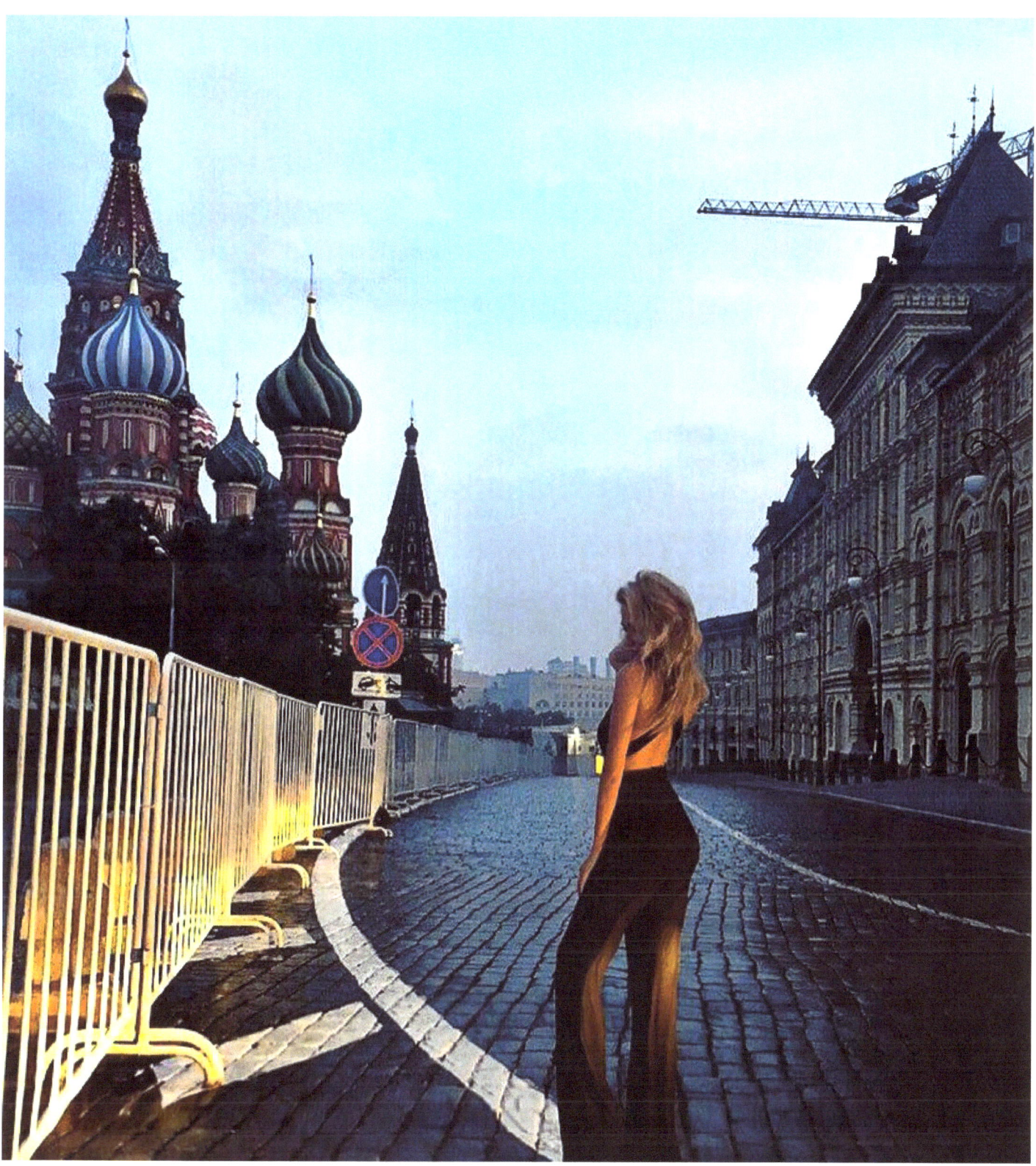

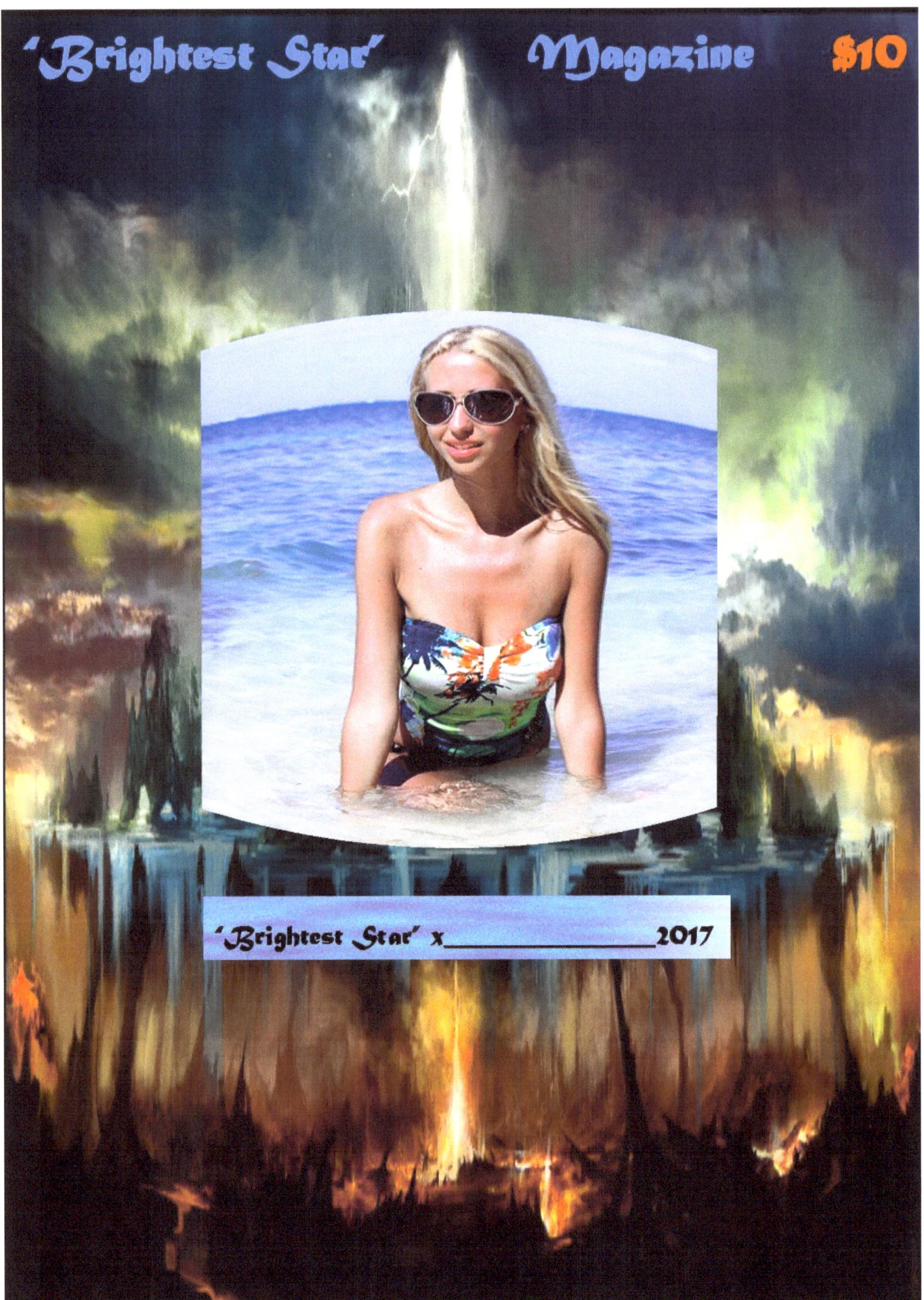

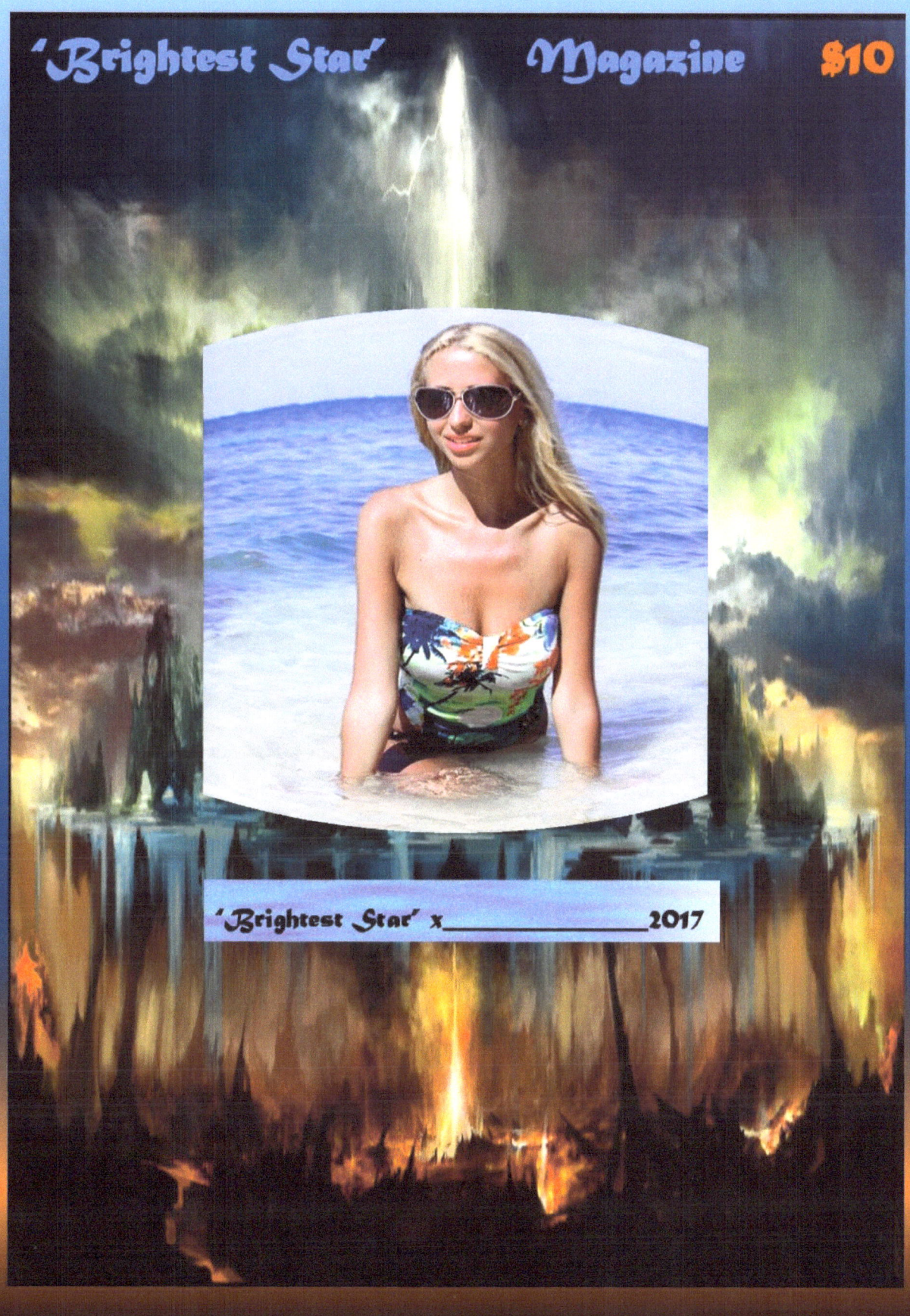

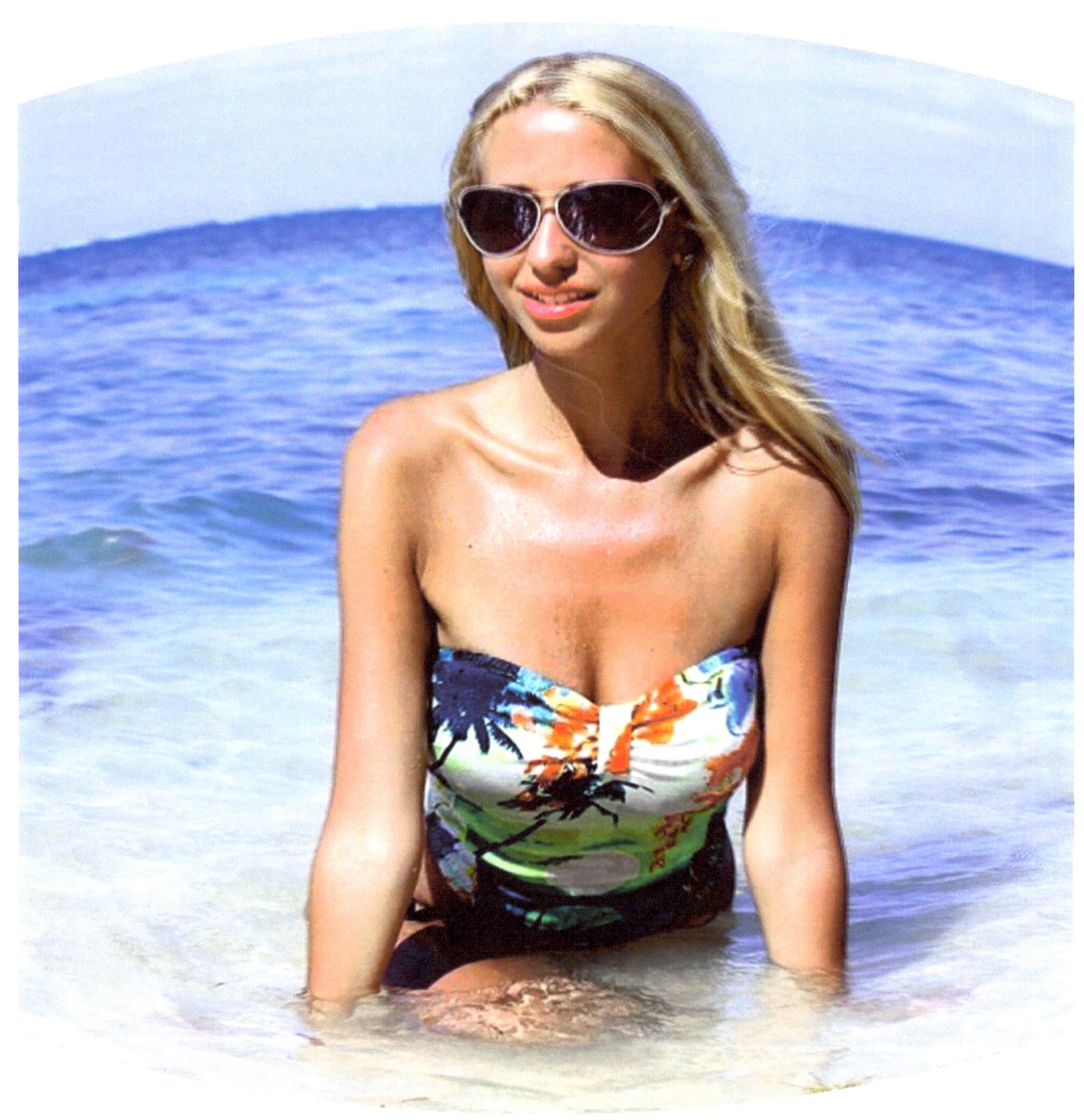

"Brightest Star" Magazine $10.00

Brightest Star Model of Ukraine

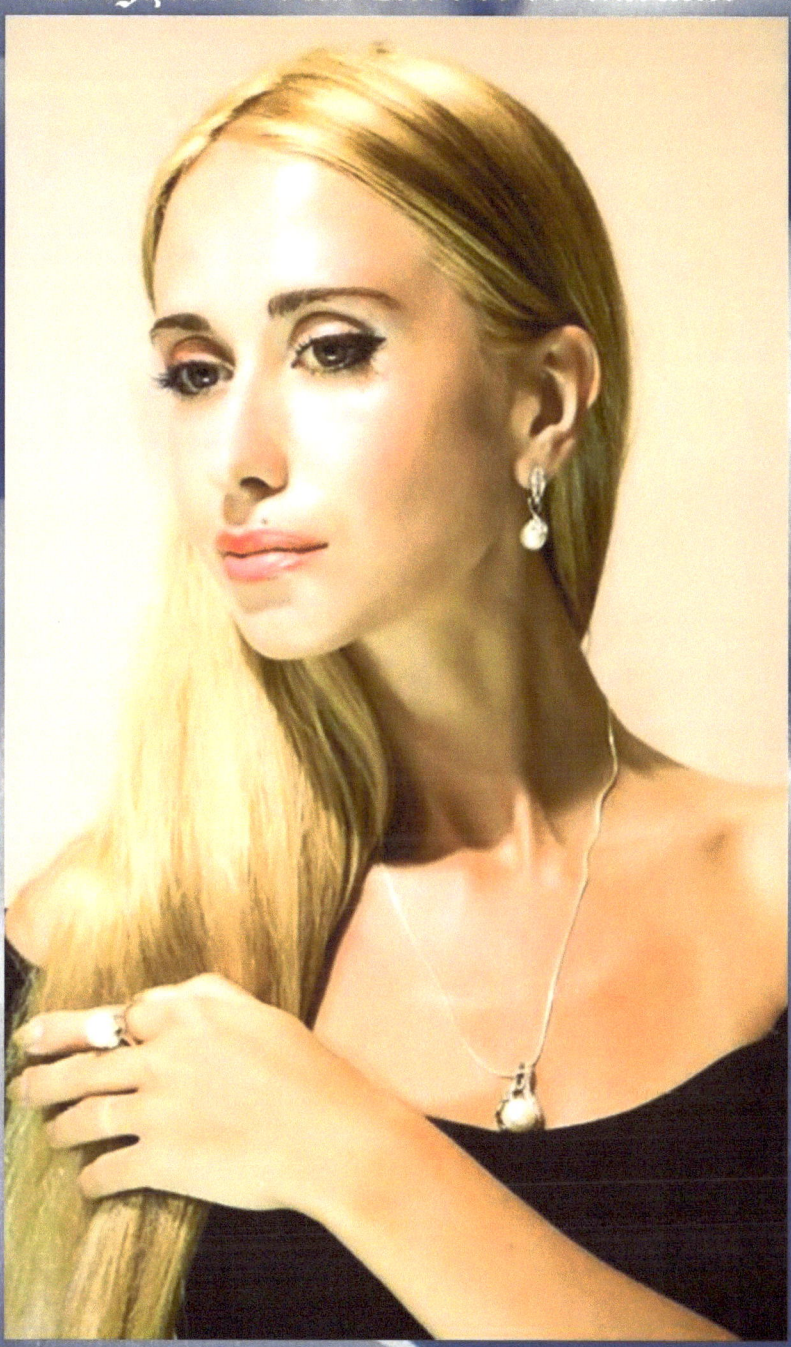

Brightest Star x_____ 2017

"Brightest Star" Magazine $10.00

****
* *

Brightest Star Model of Ukraine

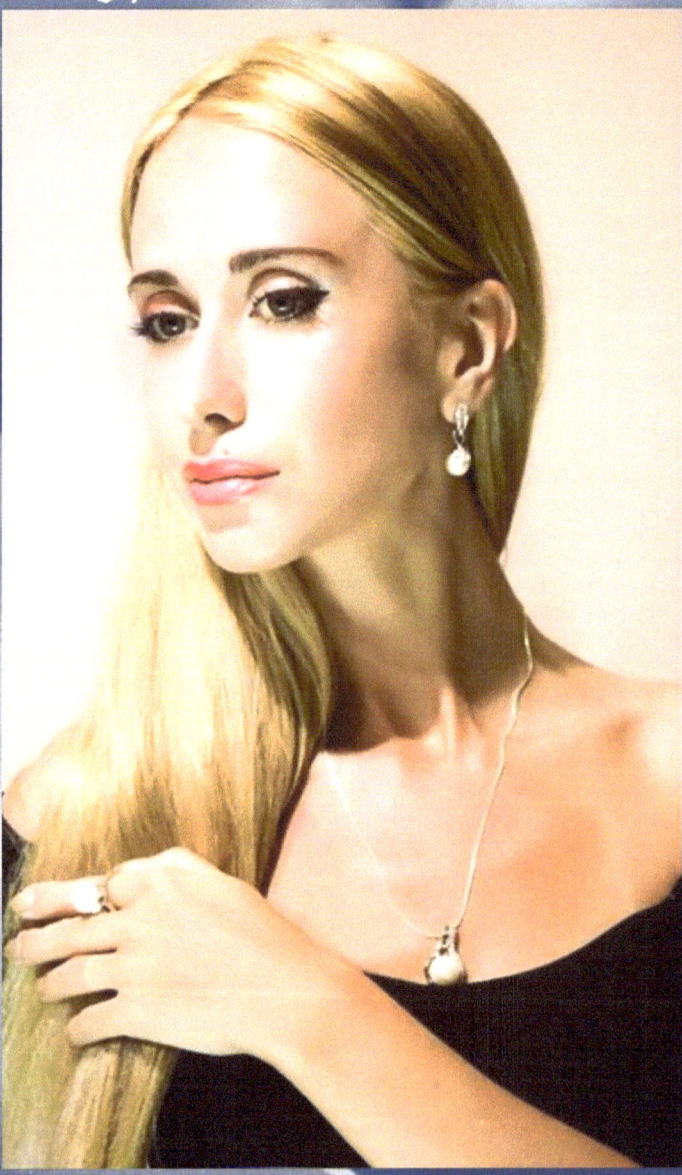

Brightest Star x_____2017

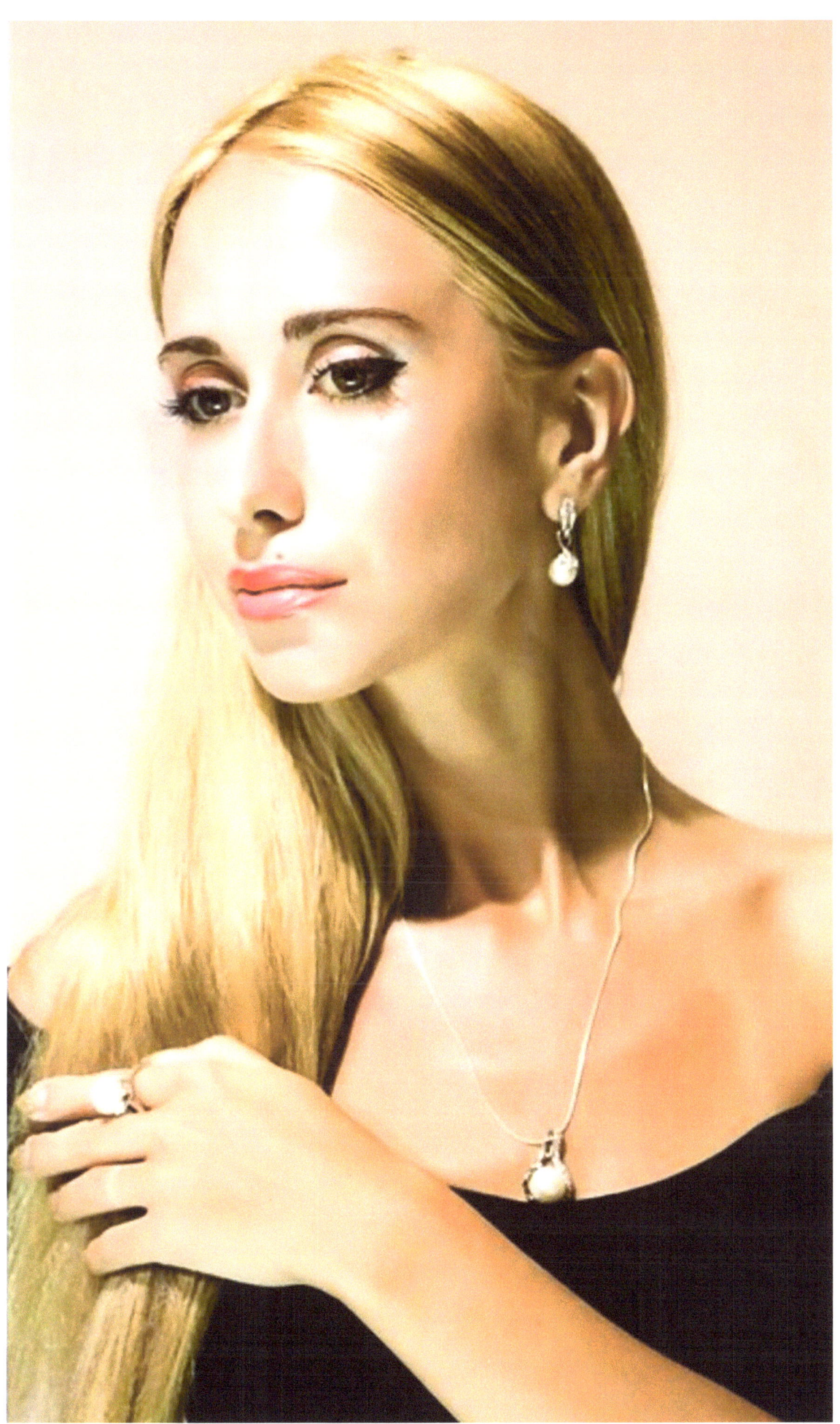

CONFIDENTIALITY

PERSONAL INFORMATION (please print or type)

Your Name: David Michael Pedger
Idea Name: "The Stealth"
Street Address: 21 Cypress Avenue
City: Shrewsbury
State/Prov: MA
Zip/Postal Code: 01545-1308
Telephone: Residence (508) 845-0042
Business ( ) Same
When is the best time to call? 24/7

BACKGROUND INFORMATION

My Idea for a New Product is...

"The Stealth" Sanitary Napkin Absorbent Pad, Centralized Quilted, by "feather" design Contoured, with "fin" to hold in place.

Creates "Stealth Sanitized"

I came up with my idea when I was...

Studying Toxic Shock Syndrome Back When People Were Dying?

(Roughly Sketch your Idea in this space)

Insert

Inner Absorbency   Quilted Lips

AGREEMENT

I believe, to the best of my knowledge, that I am the original inventor of the idea described herein. I hereby authorize Davison to provide me a no-cost discussion about my idea, with no purchase required. I understand submitting my concept is not a release and that this information cannot be used, disclosed, or sold without my expressed written permission. I also understand that all employees of Davison are required to sign an ethics and confidentiality agreement for my protection. By signing this agreement I understand that Davison does not promise or guarantee any financial gain from the development of any new product or idea.

David M. Pedge 11/3/04
Client / Date

_____ 11/3/04
Client / Date

Acknowledged by: _____ (Authorized Davison signature)

PLEASE FAX TOLL FREE OR RETURN WHITE COPY IN THE POSTAGE PAID ENVELOPE

Davison, Inc., RIDC Park, 595 Alpha Drive, Pittsburgh, PA 15238-2911   Phone: 1-800-54-IDEAS   Fax Toll Free: 1-800-540-5490

www.ingramcontent.com/pod-product-compliance
Lightning Source LLC
Chambersburg PA
CBHW040419220526
45473CB00004B/1288